KNOWledge
SUCCESSion

KNOWledge SUCCESSion

Sustained Performance and Capability Growth Through Strategic Knowledge Projects

Arthur Shelley

BUSINESS EXPERT PRESS

KNOWledge SUCCESSion: Sustained Performance and Capability Growth Through Strategic Knowledge Projects

First published in 2017 by
Business Expert Press, LLC
222 East 46th Street, New York, NY 10017
www.businessexpertpress.com

ISBN-13: 978-1-63157-158-9 (paperback)
ISBN-13: 978-1-63157-159-6 (e-book)

Business Expert Press Portfolio and Project Management Collection

Collection ISSN: 2156-8189 (print)
Collection ISSN: 2156-8200 (electronic)

Cover and interior design by Exeter Premedia Services Private Ltd., Chennai, India

First edition: 2017

10 9 8 7 6 5 4 3 2 1

Printed in the United States of America.

Abstract

KNOWledge SUCCESSion is intended for executives and developing professionals who face the challenges of delivering business benefits for today, while building the capabilities required for an increasingly changing future. The book is structured to build from foundational requirements toward connecting the highly interdependent aspects of success in an emerging complex world. A wide range of concepts are brought together in a logical framework to enable readers of different disciplines to understand how they either create barriers or can be harvested to generate synergistic opportunities. The framework builds a way to make sense of the connections and provides novel paths to take advantage of the potential synergies that arise through aligning the concepts into a portfolio of strategic projects. The insights are robust as well as pragmatic enough to equip them to ask the right questions of their project teams. It will help them to lead and coach their teams more effectively and guide them more strategically to develop the knowledge and capabilities for sustained strategic success.

This book also has extended learning for postgraduate students of business and project management in either an informal or a formal learning context. All successful medium to large organizations now need to have active management of projects and the ability to develop knowledge and capability to drive innovation and maintain relevance. There are detailed books on how to manage projects, texts of knowledge management, and volumes on innovation and change, but there is no one book that brings all these interdependent aspects of success together within the context of projects.

Keywords

business continuity, co-creation, decision making, innovation, knowledge, leadership, project leadership, project management, strategy, succession

Contents

Foreword

Over the past 100 years we have expanded the lower mental thought of logic to the higher mental thought of concepts, recognizing that patterns are key to navigating in a changing, uncertain, and complex environment. This means understanding what we don't know, what we need to know, how we come to know it, when do we need it, and what we need to do with it.

Along this road we've come to recognize that at any specific time, knowledge is not only context-sensitive and situation dependent, but also imperfect and incomplete. As individuals and organizations shift and change in a continuous coevolving loop with the environment, knowledge, too, continuously shifts and changes and expands. Through the bissociation of ideas flowing across the information highway, new ideas emerge with which other ideas can be connected. So how do we focus these amazing resources while simultaneously enabling the emergence of future ideas necessary for sustainability?

Arthur Shelley has his ear to the pulse of the organizational zoo, bringing high-level theory down to the ground and understanding the way people learn is experiential. Ten years of neuroscience research collated in our book, *Expanding the Self: The Intelligent Complex Adaptive Learning System,* offers an expanded experiential learning model that adds the fifth mode of social engagement. Within the frame of bounded projects, KNOWledge SUCCESSion brings that model to life, engaging collaborative experts to focus on the *why* and *what*, and letting the *how* emerge and co-evolve with the future.

When Arthur first introduced KNOWledge SUCCESSion, I assumed it was about Leadership. Then I kept hearing about the significance of a project focus. Then, I heard ideas that addressed knowledge attrition in organizations. Okay, so now that I've read it and reflected, it's about all of those things ... AND it's ALL about knowledge sharing. It's no surprise that **KS,** the acronym that represents Knowledge Sharing, is also the acronym representing **KNOWledge SUCCESSion!** Before the turn of the century in the U.S. Department of the Navy, we shifted our perception from knowledge is power to *Knowledge Shared Is Power Squared*. Yet, 20 years later, we still have individuals and organizations who *don't get it*. When knowledge is shared, it opens the door to a creative and innovative future.

The societal, political, and environmental forces at work today simultaneously challenge us and offer an unprecedented opportunity for change. Forces grow when one part of a system creates in a very different way than another part of a system. Within the organizational setting, space and time are often separated, with decision makers acting from different agendas rather than pursuing a connectedness of choices. Knowledge sharing is a critical factor in bringing space and time together. For example, within a specific domain of knowledge, communities of practice facilitate the discovery of solutions across functional areas and organizations, negating geographical or bureaucratic boundaries. Similarly, embracing the strategic power of projects, **KNOWledge SUCCESSion** connects current and future decision makers with the knowledge of today and tomorrow, spanning the boundary of time, weaving a thread of continuity without limiting project outcomes to the incomplete knowledge of today.

Ultimately, knowledge is all about action. The actions taken today impact the actions taken tomorrow. KNOWledge SUCCESSion provides a roadmap for taking actions today to achieve sustained performance and capability growth through strategic knowledge projects. *Action with traction ensures satisfaction.*

Dr. Alex Bennet

Mountain Quest Institute

Former Chief of Knowledge, U.S. Navy

Acknowledgments

This book could not have been written without applying the techniques it describes. That is, co-creation of new knowledge through conversations. During the two years this book was being developed, there have been many conversations with too many people to name individually and I am grateful to all who have engaged in these mutual learning interactions. Conversations with members of AuSKM, Melbourne KM Leadership Forum, SIKM Leaders, and The Organizational Zoo Ambassadors Network have been the stimulating fuel for knowledge co-creation throughout the development of this book.

Special thanks to the following contributors who invested time and effort to provide mini case studies to add richness to the insights to this book. Your contributions are appreciated and enrich the content.

Vishnupriya Sengupta (PWC, India), Vincent Ribiere (IKISEA, Thailand), Ricky Tsui (Arup University, Singapore), Randhir Pushpa (Unisys, India), Alex Bennet (Mountain Quest Institute, USA), Bill Kaplan (Working Knowledge, USA), Keith De La Rue (Acknowledge Consulting, Australia), Paul Culmsee (Seven Sigma, Australia), James Price (Experience Matters, Australia), Aaron A. Palileo (Bootleg Innovation Design, Philippines), Stuart French (Delta Knowledge, Australia), Brigitte Carbonneau (Cirque du Soleil, Canada), and Joseph Howard and Juan Roman (NASA, USA). Thanks to Mark Boyes for the creative artworks to stimulate knowledge co-creation conversations.

The book is more professional as a result of the support of Cath Shelley of Intelligent Answers and the arduous and excellent editorial work of Tanya Hunter. It is not an easy task to bring together my divergent thoughts into a flowing book such as this and your guidance helped enormously.

Thanks also go to Dr. Michael Sutton, for challenges, comments, and feedback throughout the writing process and his postscript, which provides a creative insight. Dr. Alex Bennet's understanding of interdependent complexities have also been a great help in connecting concepts in this book and her opening foreword sets the context for the future challenge we all face.

I am grateful to Tim Kloppenberg of Business Expert Press for inviting me to write this book after several conversations about what people need to know to be successful in our modern projectized world.

Optimizing Value from This Book

Greater learning occurs when the ideas from this book are discussed in open dialogue with trusted peers and leaders. Reflecting on the concepts can be enhanced by using the end of chapter questions and the mini-case studies to explore how they can apply in your own context and to gain a wide range of perspectives in group discussions. You can also explore deeper insights by referring to the extended references list for this book at www.IntelligentAnswers.com.au/KNOWledgeSUCCESSion

CHAPTER 1

KNOWledge SUCCESSion for Performance

Executive Summary

This chapter sets the context for the book and highlights why strategic project portfolios are critical to ongoing performance (for individuals, teams, organizations, and across organizational networks).

Key points of this chapter are:

- Projects are the new "business as usual" for progressive organizations and perceptions of success vary over time and between stakeholders.
- Operational models for organizations need to engage in continuous change and redevelopment of knowledge to remain viable and relevant.
- Projects are the optimal mechanism to deliver short- and long-term benefits to enable ongoing relevance and competitive advantage.

KNOWledge SUCCESSion for performance involves understanding the connections between:

1. Knowing, KNOWledge SUCCESSion, and sustained performance.
2. Business as usual or projectization?
3. Strategic projects as vehicles of knowledge transfer.
4. Leave your tacit knowledge at the door when you go.
5. Knowledge, projects, context, and sense-making.

Knowing, Knowledge SUCCESSion, and Sustained Performance

The biggest challenge faced by many organizations is creating and maintaining a knowledge base that would keep the organization at its optimal performance. Global economies, like trust, take significant time to build but can crash in moments. Our complex and highly interdependent modern environment requires us to be in a constant state of sensemaking to perceive how we are tracking and how to manage the emergent changes thrust upon us.[1]

Figure 1.1 is a metaphorical depiction of a modern work environment. When people are asked how this image relates to their organization they engage in divergent conversations about what it represents, some positive, some negative, all insightful reflections.

Competitive advantage does not automatically flow from simply knowing more than others; it requires application of that knowledge faster and more efficiently and effectively than anyone else in your industry or others. Everyone knows what it takes to live a healthier lifestyle—eat less and exercise more! That we KNOW this that counts less than whether we can act on it effectively. Whether you are a commercial enterprise, in government, or a not-for-profit, being the best and doing the right things at the right times requires constant reflection and a forward-focused strategic plan.

Figure 1.1 Knowledge flows recycle and adapt through the environment

What Is KNOWledge SUCCESSion?

The way we interact with each other significantly impacts our success. To KNOW SUCCESS in a sustainable manner, individuals, teams, and organizations need to actively manage their KNOWledge SUCCESSion. We must understand what we need to know, how we come to know it, when we need it, and what we need to unlearn or adapt for future application.

KNOW*ledge* SUCCESS*ion* (KS) is a new strategy for achieving optimal performance in a world of emergent complexity. More than just capture or transfer of knowledge, KS combines many interdependent aspects of knowledge to create synergies and align actions with overall organizational strategy. KS is depicted in Figure 1.2 as social interactions based on conversations, stories, and shared insights that lead to inclusive interactions. These are connected through constant attention by questioning why actions are being taken and what value they create (both tangible and intangible), that is, directly aligned with the goals of the person, team, or organization. This approach leads to reflective constructive challenges that start with why and end with a carefully considered portfolio of projects that deliver immediate project outputs and create the foundations for future success. Thus, KS becomes the driver of innovation and capability development and, ultimately, sustainable performance.

KS refers to the co-creation, transfer, and application of knowledge in short-term cycles to stimulate value creation and experiential learning. In doing so, it builds foundations, insights, and capabilities for the next

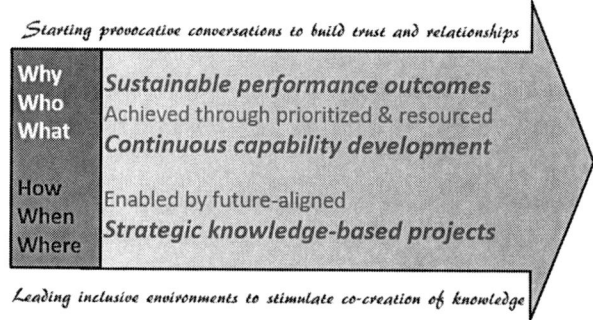

Figure 1.2 The social and logical aspects of knowledge flows that lead to KNOWledge SUCCESSion

stages of organization evolution. KS requires both leadership and management. Leadership must engage others around a common future path and show followers why the priorities chosen represent this optimal path. Management must set the priorities and jettison less important initiatives that may distract effort and drain resources. Successful people and organizations have moved away from a traditional world of "this OR that" to our current contexts of "this AND that." Often seemingly contradictory actions may run in parallel, exploring multiple options to find the best path. These simultaneous actions generate new insights so that we learn rapidly and develop the next cycle of parallel initiatives. Prioritizing the initiatives that generate the most value is critical because spreading valued knowledge resources across too many activities will also result in failure.[2]

How Does It work?

In short, **KNOW***ledge* **SUCCESS***ion* provides a means to know and experience success in iterative experiential fragments rather than rigidly plan for long periods. The short cycles remain aligned with the longer vision, but both short- and long-term goals are more flexible than in traditional structures. For example, when hiring new talent, the standard process was to have a very clear description of the qualifications and role. However, now we are more likely to seek someone capable of learning quickly and being highly adaptable, because medium- and long-term roles will likely change. **KS** philosophy is a more agile and iterative approach than traditional ways of working. It takes an ongoing capability development view of all actions, rather than just the immediate delivery objectives. It thus reverses the traditional approach of every detail in advance and allows emergence to include new knowledge as the process proceeds. It maintains a focus on delivering agreed tangible outputs while enabling the process to adjust during the project. This is not completely new, as some organizations have a history of this approach. For example, NASA did not know if or how "landing a man on the moon and returning him safely to the earth" was possible when challenged to do so by President John F. Kennedy in 1961. NASA experts had to rapidly develop their capabilities to deliver this stated objective, despite a lack of knowledge on how. At least they had a clearly stated vision! It would have been much easier to land on the moon and not worry about safe return. However, in the absence of KNOWledge SUCCESSion, NASA has since "forgotten" how to accomplish this remarkable feat.[3]

In many ways, our entire world is like this challenge to NASA, except we are now expected to do such tasks on shorter timeframes and with fewer resources. Very few organizations have the longer-term vision of how they will look in a decade, or even if they will still exist. Despite this, very long-term projects still get done. The military still develops and builds new equipment, such as fleets of diversified ships, which take decades to complete. Rarely is anyone present from the beginning of such projects to completion. So every position and role within the lifetime of that project has been handed over to a new person, or even several people.

This highlights why **KNOW***ledge* **SUCCESS***ion* is so important. The ability to pass on lessons learned as the project proceeds is fundamental to success. Continuous co-creation and exchange of knowledge and insights fuels innovation and builds relationships. This in turn drives engagement and motivation leading to success. Hagel and Brown[4] described continuous innovation through the development of specialized capabilities as the ultimate way to drive competitive advantage. The way we interact and how long we maintain our connections determine whether this is likely to occur in our environment. Trusted relationships are the foundation of what gets shared and what does not, and the behavioral environment is set by what we do, not what we say. Leaders are (should be) positive role models and people can choose whether to follow based on how leaders and their actions are perceived. A leader whose behavior contradicts what they ask their followers to do is like a parent who smokes cigarettes or drinks alcohol telling their child not to. Such leaders sacrifice credibility and will be judged as hypocrites. Genuine leaders have ***willing, intelligent*** followers: Willing because the followers buy into their leader's vision, and intelligent because followers have actively considered their leader's ideas, actions, and credibility and committed to the leader's vision. That is, they follow because they consciously and ethically choose to, not because they are forced down a path through control and command compliance.[5]

What Are the Benefits of KS?

KNOW*ledge* **SUCCESS***ion* recognizes that we willingly share our knowledge and insights with those we trust and respect. It is a process of interactive exchange that stimulates new ideas and becomes a self-perpetuating cycle in which people feel valued. They are engaged and secure and unafraid to "bounce" something untried. Ideas and concepts are nurtured to a point where they are robust enough to justify themselves, but not so much that the strategically weaker ones survive. The Darwinian evolution concept of "adapt or die" ensures that the most robust innovations arise in the shortest possible time. Evolving WITH the environment as it changes makes **KS** a powerful concept. It facilitates an emergent pathway that allows people to learn rapidly from their own mistakes, and the mistakes of others, thus providing a greater resilience to external forces.

Leading an environment that facilitates **KS** is largely about the behavior of leaders and the behaviors that leaders inspire and encourage within their teams. Supporting fast, cheap failure to learn quickly is a feature of the "safe-fail" environment.[6] Encouraging appropriate risk taking to drive innovation and rewarding learning guarantees that shared ideas accelerate the transfer and reapplication of knowledge. Knowledge recycling fuels creativity, invention, and innovation just as cash flow fuels the economy. If all knowledge is frozen in the minds of a few, this impedes the flow of knowledge and the potential value it creates. Capture of knowledge is not the key to success—releasing it is! Knowledge must be released internally so it can be amplified, reapplied, reworked, and adapted for new contexts. Sometimes, it needs renovation or decommissioning because newer and better knowledge has been created and can be more productively leveraged across people during role transitions. Those who believe that "knowledge is power" have never experienced the exhilaration of seeing that "knowledge is powerful when shared, socialized, adapted and reapplied." We greatly amplify our impact and the value we create when we trust others[7] with our knowledge and invest time exploring how we collectively leverage it. We keep knowledge flowing though value-generating cycles by nurturing an open and collaborative environment.

What Are the Challenges?

Ironically, open sharing of knowledge is something that we are taught to avoid throughout our lives. In fact, throughout most Western education systems we are punished for sharing or being creative about how we use or adapt knowledge.[8] You can't copy or benefit from what your fellow student does. You can't tell them what your ideas are as that is considered to be cheating. You must write the number in the box, color between the lines, or paint according to the coded numbers to generate a standardized result. It should be no surprise that "educated people" emerging from this system are not very good at sharing when they arrive in the workplace! The system has removed interactivity and creativity and generated homogeneous graduates who can recite facts, without a deep understanding of what facts mean, why they are important, or how to act on them.

Some learning facilitators are taking a different approach, more aligned with KS. In postgraduate knowledge courses I have designed and facilitated, everything is different. Students are rewarded for helping other students, because that is what we want in the workplace. Assignments are completed in open wiki environments, so students learn for each other and collectively generate a database that is both robust and relevant to work contexts and capabilities. In this way, the overall standard is raised for everyone. Students are exposed to wider and richer knowledge-sharing experience, and this collaborative experiential learning builds student's capabilities well beyond what each learns individually. These courses are popular and highly rated by participants, not because they are easy, but because they challenge students and provide freedom to explore what is valuable for their future. Although guided by past knowledge, they come to understand how to generate insights about unknown future scenarios. They enjoy the exhilaration of co-creation, discovery, and reflecting on how what they are learning can be applied to THEIR real world. Inspiring others to share and transfer knowledge can be influenced more by what you reject, than by what you attempt to control. Learning is about opening minds, not filling them.

This approach to co-creative and active learning applies equally well in organizations as in optimal formal learning. Organizational leaders can demonstrate their commitment to the **KS approach** by doing it them-selves. They can:

- ask, instead of tell;
- acknowledge the benefits of learning when errors are made;
- constructively critique successes to see if they could have been better; and
- admit and reflect upon their own errors.

Such leaders are more likely to be admired and respected by behaving this way, than by pretending to be something they are not. Building a culture like this does not happen overnight. Humans, being both social and competitive by nature, can be complex to deal with and quite unpredictable. Behavioral and cultural changes require patience, persistence, and commitment to overcome the impacts of those who want to "play the game." People focused on their own short-term benefits rather than mutual value exchange will fight to maintain the status quo, because they are afraid constructive changes toward a KS culture reduces their self-benefits. This does not have to be true. The KS approach will benefit everyone more, though these benefits will be more evenly shared.

One example of a KS-aligned co-creation approach to simplify behavioral interactions is to use a metaphor like *The Organizational Zoo.*[9] Rather than tell people what their stereotypical culture is, the approach allows workshop participants co-create their own assessment through conversation and card games that make it easier to visualize behaviors and their impacts on interactions. This unique and creative approach engages people to represent each behavior as an animal character and to explore the impacts each has on the other animals (behaviors) in the zoo. Most people do not have advanced skills in psychology and do not understand the details of many psychometric profilers. People often feel "categorized" by such tools, which can limit what they think their options are. *The Organizational Zoo* concept differs because it focuses on which "animals" are most appropriate for the given context, highlighting that people choose behavior proactively instead of being forced to react in defined ways.[10] Once participants understand that they can create the behavioral environment that is most likely to generate their desired outcomes, their own behavior and actions change through heightened awareness and self-reflection.

Outcomes?

Constructive conversations help us realize that behavior is not just about individuals, it is about how people work together in each particular context. Metaphor helps us to understand complex situations and to engage with each other on how we can approach uncertainty.[11] When we discuss a range of options offered by people with different perspectives, we come to understand that our own view is just one possibility among many. While we may not agree with all offered perspectives, at least we become aware of them. We can make a more informed choice about how we behave to achieve the optimal outcomes, providing us with a greater chance of success. When we don't engage in conversations about the impacts of behavior and what is best for each situation, failure is more likely. We can decide to be inspirational, creative, and collaborative when brainstorming. Then we can deliberately adjust our behavior to be controlling, critical, and task focused when we prioritize our list of creative ideas into actionable initiatives. Consciously adjusting behaviors to align with context generates better outcomes and more value.

So KNOWledge SUCCESSion provides us with the ability to KNOW SUCCESS in a sustainable way by strategically building the knowledge and capability to actively adapt and retain competitive advantage. Understanding the highly interdependent nature of knowledge and behavior is just one element of this approach. This book explores how other factors intertwine in complex ways to challenge how well we attract the funding and attention we need to remain operational and successful. Focusing on one aspect of knowing and doing is insufficient. Optimal performance is the outcome of dealing with complex factors all together, even though they often appear to be in conflict. Optimal choices integrate a range of complex interdependencies and find synergies, rather than allow them to drive divisions, frustrations, and conflict.

Business as Usual or Projectization?

In the past few decades, organizations have almost entirely flipped from being process driven to project driven. This is a result of the accelerating globalization of organizations and dynamic changes in knowledge and technology. By the time something is invented and developed into a working product or service, it is often almost obsolete or at least changed in fundamental design. Several decades of rapid change have created an almost insatiable hunger for newer, faster, better products or services. This means that innovation projects must be implemented more quickly than in the past, and done in more flexible ways such as the Agile approach: "Processes enable us to maintain status quo and projects are the way we implement change for the future."[12]

In the past, organizations that were more efficient performed well. This generated a focus on "best practice" and inward small changes to make the product as efficiently (cost focus) and effectively (quality fit for purpose focus) as possible. This approach to operation is very effective in most organizations; IF we assume that their business environment and customer and consumer needs remain the same. Very well-documented and detailed processes are critical to some elements of business such as safety, financial policy, and systems control, as these do not need to change dramatically in the short term and a high degree of control is appropriate. However, a focus on remaining the same with tightly controlled processes can be less effective in a rapidly changing environment, or even a competitive disadvantage.

Our current reality, whether in not-for-profit or for-profit organizations, is that the parameters we operate under are constantly changing and the future is increasingly less certain. This requires a different style of leadership and management and impacts how we value knowledge and how we blend strategy and tactics. Inevitably, in conditions of uncertainty, tactical reactions are applied more as people are unsure of what actions may be appropriate beyond the immediate situation. While this is appropriate during a crisis, it is not a robust long-term strategy.[13] The ultimate outcome of the new reality is that decision makers are more inclined to manage what they can control and leave the rest until they know more about what options apply. This is largely because decision makers are measured and rewarded based on relatively short-term results and often engaged on short-term contracts. Such an approach creates a constant self-perpetuating crisis as longer-term strategic development investments are forever delayed, while resources are overinvested in reactionary problem solving.

The more stable environment of the past enabled thorough planning of the occasional development project. Past projects either enhanced existing systems and processes, or replaced them through commissioning a new solution while phasing out the old. The challenge of such implementation is that many projects exceed the life expectancy of the new product or service generated. This is why failure rates are so high for complex projects.[14] While there are successful longer-term projects, especially in military and large government infrastructure programs, these too often are challenged by changing requirements during implementation; fueled by changing social norms and demographics, as well as shifting political and social trends.[15]

Because of the factors mentioned before (and other interdependent aspects of our modern world), successful organizations have become "projectized" (also referred to as Projectification). While not a real word (yet), it has become a common spoken term in conversations describing business approaches dealing with complexity and uncertainty. A projectized organization is one that operates primarily through projects rather than ongoing standardized procedures. A much higher proportion of people in such organizations are engaged in project work, and many people are contracted for specific "pieces of unique work" in projects rather than repeatable routines. Business as usual has migrated from unchanging processes into a portfolio of projects with little remaining the same from year to year. Although some back-office support functions remain fundamentally unchanged, many of these are being automated or outsourced as they are seen to be generic functions that do not contribute to competitive advantage. Keeping them in-house is often seen by the decision makers as not of core value or inefficient. This is often a mistake as it prioritizes tactical responses over building a strategic foundation of capabilities.

The perceived solution? Implement a series of projects that deliver the latest tactical desired outcome. This is often followed by another series of projects that reverse the previous ones, resulting in cycles of outsourcing and insourcing. Similarly cycles of downsizing, right-sizing, and upsizing go often in harmony (or disharmony) with globalization, regionalization, and separation. Attention and resources are often so focused on managing the change projects that one wonders how the real value in the business gets generated. The expression "the tail wagging the dog" is commonly heard in reference to this.

Amid all this chaos, there are some organizations that have become completely projectized. Some of these even offer their strategic project and change expertise as a part of core services to other businesses as a revenue-generation stream. There is a growing market for this, as many organizations struggle to make the transition from traditional silo structure to completely matrix. The majority of large successful businesses now have a mix of functional silos (for traditional and back-office activities) and cross-organization matrix structures that focus on delivery of change through projects. This blended organization is more adapted to the unpredictable environment that most of us now face.

In the projectized organization, strategy has become the delivery of a series of aligned projects. In well-led and managed organizations, these projects collectively determine the strategic direction of the organization, and projects deliver organizational goals in annual cycles (or in the best examples in significantly longer cycles). Some examples of completely projectized organizations that have evolved well to perform at the highest levels in this environment include Fluor, Arup, Siemens, Tata, and Parsons. The striking thing about these organizations is their total focus on project delivery and delivery for other clients on large contractual undertakings. The projects can be from any stage of the business cycle ranging from research, creating demand, design, marketing, sales, procurement, construction, implementation, commissioning, decommissioning, outsourcing, or onboarding. Although the organizations mentioned have more experience in large infrastructure projects, other smaller specialist project management consultancies provide services across all imaginable industries and at both frontline functions and back-office support services.

One of the outcomes of these changes over time is it has become difficult to imagine an effective business professional who does not have strong project management understanding. This means not just knowing how to manage the internal workings of projects and the supporting systems such as PM BOK or commercial PM methodologies such as Prince2, it means understanding how to decide which projects need to be done and why these are the ones most aligned with strategic performance. Prioritization (discussed in detail later) is a key capability for performance of many organizations, and this will separate successful future leaders from those that follow trends. The ability to make better-informed decisions in times of uncertainty can be luck (occasionally), but those with more effective ways to solicit insights earlier and act on them will dominate. The shift from process focus to project orientation has already changed how organizations operate. We now need to focus on what this means for the capabilities needed for both personal knowledge and the collective knowledge of organizations. This includes the knowledge people need to apply, how they make sense of this knowledge, and when it does and does not apply, especially in fluid situations.

Strategic Projects as Vehicles of Knowledge Transfer

"When nothing is changing, you can continue to do what you have always done and be successful, but that is not the context in which the ambitious person now finds themselves." A key challenge is *how can you know what you know, when you need to know it?* With every project implemented, there is knowledge of what was; that may no longer be true, and knowledge of new systems, processes, tools, and relationships that need to be assimilated and understood before the new context delivered by that project can made effective. This implies that the project itself becomes the vehicle of the change required. That is much more than just the physical aspects of the change (the new software or process, the bridge over the river, the satellite in space, or the replacement of all televisions when digital communication was introduced). Far more important are knowledge and understanding of how our processes, decisions, and interactions need to change to optimize the impacts of the project. This knowledge has implications on behavioral and social aspects at individual, team, and organizational levels and sometimes well beyond your individual organization.

When Apple released the first smart phone, the company completely changed the dynamics of several industries and caused market leaders in industries other than its own to change, as well as changed the way people across the planet interacted with each other. A significant part of Apple's success was having an intuitive way for their consumers both to understand the potential of their new product and to provide the knowledge to easily adjust to this (both technically and socially). The adoption of social media and leverage of community identities was extremely well implemented, right from the beginning of the project. Rather than just focus on needs, Apple went beyond expectations and delivered desires that consumers did not know they had. In doing so, Apple raised the bar for everyone who wanted to play in a range of markets (telecommunications, computing, social media, mobile technology, on-line sales, and more). This also opened opportunities for new players with different knowledge and created industries to satisfy these new demands (such as the development of mobile applications and the explosion of other intuitive mobile innovations). The most amazing aspect of how Apple approached this innovation project was that they did not invent much new technology. They simply recombined many existing concepts into a new combined format and made it interesting and engaging for their stakeholders to assimilate; a lesson most projects could learn.

It was almost as if Apple invented the perfect "change project pill"; a medication that immediately instilled all knowledge required to effectively use the products and services associated with the project and a desire to adopt it. Imagine a world of projects where millions of stakeholders across many languages and cultures are literally lining up at your door, eagerly anticipating the project "go-live." Certainly not typical of most projects in most organizations. So what are we doing wrong?

The world of project management has more failures than successes, and the literature is littered with stories of disasters and lessons (not) learned.[16] Paradoxically, there are organizations that deliver far higher success rates than the average for project delivery. What do they do and know that others do not? Clearly, projects are challenging and all organizations have underdelivered on some, but a key difference between consistent high performers and lower performers is that high performers work through knowledge and capability development cycles. Better anticipation, prioritization, and learning are common denominators in highly professional project organizations such as Arup, Fluor, and Tata. Each of these organizations has deliberate and focused efforts to build knowledge and project management capabilities as part of the delivery of the projects themselves. That is, the project is a learning opportunity and capabilities developed are then adapted and reapplied across future projects. Retention of knowledge goes well beyond content and reports to proactively cultivate networks and opportunities to socialize and constructively challenge. This requires a special culture of continuous improvement and projects as strategic building blocks well beyond the immediate project. In such environments, people welcome other perspectives and understand that creative friction is productive for all involved.[17]

Figure 1.3 highlights a generic cycle that connects these interdependent activities that takes us beyond a project to a strategic project that produces promised benefits for the immediate project stakeholders while developing knowledge and capabilities to leverage over time for a sustained competitive advantage. This goes well beyond the "Iron Triangle" of time (schedule), scope (functionality), cost (resources), and quality

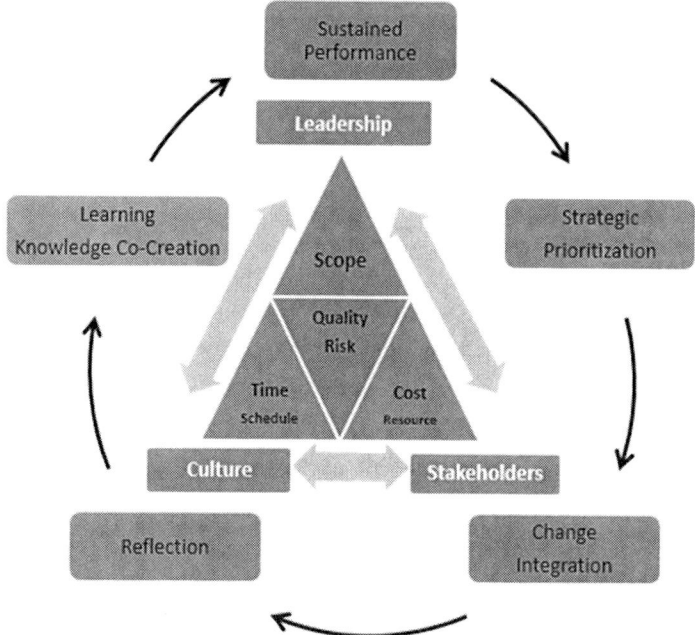

Figure 1.3 Knowledge flow and application through strategic project cycles to sustain performance

(standard expected). The iron triangle remains at the heart of success-ful project delivery, but is just an integral part of a wider set of aspects. Around these more tactical and tangible elements of delivering successful projects are the more intangible and strategic aspects. A successful project leader understands that they optimize their own performance, as well as that of their team and the organization as a whole, by balancing all of these interdependent components. Note the flow of knowledge through the stages is triggered and completed by verbs (action). That is, it not sufficient to have the knowledge; it needs to be applied at the right time and in the right context to optimize performance.

There is a time to think divergently to create ideas and options and a time to focus the conversations and converge on the best options to ensure costs are not overrun and resources stretched. Too many organizations do not balance these well. Some remain in strategy development without implementing projects to generate value, and others rapidly act in a tacti-cal manner without connecting their projects to secure synergies between them. The flow of knowledge across projects is often more important for sustained performance, than the flow within a project. However, both are more difficult to harvest in times of high turnover and contracted project environments. Although it appears cheaper to separate projects and it is easier to measure them, this approach can negatively impact overall per-formance because it misses the potential cross-pollination and disrupts knowledge flows.

Projects can be the vehicle through which each step toward achieving strategic goals is delivered in a continuing and highly interdependent set of actions over time. Each project needs to satisfy its specific outputs while aligning with the overall program and stimulating a sense of stra-tegic purpose for those involved. In environments with a common sense of purpose, engagement levels are high and this impacts performance and loyalty,[18] thereby supporting the ongoing growth and success.

A project, like building a house, is focused on the delivery of the agreed outputs within the boundaries of the agreed inputs (all very quan-titative, objective, and convergent to achieve predictability within the defined timeline). A program of strategic projects, like raising a family in the home, is much more qualitative, subjective, divergent, and emergent, well beyond the predictable timeline. Projects are managed in isolation because it is easier to manage and measure them that way. While costs are incurred before and during the project as outputs are delivered, the more important outcomes (value and intangible benefits) are continuously generated AFTER the project is completed,[19] that is, when the outputs of the project are put to use and people start interacting with each other when using it.

Some projects considered a disaster at their time of completion have generated far more value than their cost (such as the Sydney Opera House), whereas others considered a "project success" have been a commercial disaster (such as the Sydney Harbour Tunnel). More realistic measures of project success need to be considered across a wider social context and over a longer period of time if we are to get better at delivering the right projects in the right way. Some informed organizations are looking to measure the performance of projects, not only on the delivery of the immediate tasks, but also on the longer-term outcomes from the project.

This chapter sets the context for the book and highlights why to KNOW SUCCESS through modern projects requires a strategic approach to KNOWledge SUCCESSion. Another of our paradoxical challenges is that we simply cannot afford to relearn with each project we embark upon and, at the same time, we cannot assume that what we already know will continue to apply to future project contexts.

Leave Your Tacit Knowledge at the Door When You Go

I recall a pilot project in an international environment where what was learned was diligently collated and passed on to the next stage of development through a series of files. The pilot project manager then invested time and effort to meet with those involved in the next phase to ensure that the next team understood the implications of the learning and to provide insights on how to optimize the program going forward. When the pilot project manager arrived, the beneficiaries of this advice were too busy kicking off the next stage to meet with him and stated they did not have the time to go over the documentation. The opportunity for knowledge transfer and learning was lost, and many of the errors that were highlighted by the pilot project manager were not prevented. Higher costs were incurred and time to completion was slower than if the advice had been adopted. This is often referred to as "not invented here syndrome" and is far more common than it needs to be.

It does not take long to consider prior learning points and decide which of these might enable the next project (or phase of a program) to be adjusted based on these insights. The two most common complaints about "Lessons Learned" processes or systems are (1) those finishing up a project do not take them seriously (not sharing ideas or paying lip service to the documentation) and (2) lessons learned are not used for a discovery process before starting a project. This is a cultural issue well beyond what is covered in basic project management literature focused on single projects. It is an unfortunate outcome of measuring projects on measures that pertain only within the project itself. Until project measures and bonuses have components based on the outcomes (delivery of longer-term benefits) rather than outputs (on-time and budget delivery, regardless of readiness of the organization to utilize the solution), this culture is unlikely to change.

The justifiable challenge to outcomes measures and payments is that there are too many factors that impact longer-term outcomes that are beyond the influence of the project manager (or contract provider). These are indicated in the outer cycle in Figure 1.3 and influenced by subjective and social factors such as politics, stakeholders outside the project team, organizational support for the project, and how well the organization has prioritized. Organizations commonly have long lists of "priority 1" projects, many of which do not have a detailed resource allocation plan. This all-too-familiar situation makes it almost impossible to secure the resources required at the optimal time to deliver on your project. This should be highlighted as a significant risk on projects, but is too often accepted as normal, though less common in higher-performing organizations.

"The key point is that people learn, not organizations." The Learning Organization concept is an excellent theoretical concept, which is realized through engaging people to stay and share. Knowledge is created and exchanged through trusted relationships and fostering social interactions through forums, communities of practice, mentoring, innovation forums, and other means where people explore, exchange, and develop ideas. Projects are the perfect opportunity for this as they provide close working relationships required for trust and the context in which colleagues can explore real challenges that impact on their ability to achieve. Vested mutual interest in a team environment generates optimal learning for each individual and the team. However, much of this is lost when teams are temporary. Organizations that do not have continuity across projects have to rebuild the relationships to develop the trust to enable the constructive conversations that build the knowledge. This pathway is broken in project organizations with high employee or contractor turnover, and these organizations underperform as a result. However, the opposite can also be an issue. When there is little or no turnover of people, cross-fertilization of ideas and diversity of experiences are reduced, leading to greater group think and less innovation. If we attempt to simplify projects so they are easily measured and managed, we miss the synergies. However, if we make them too complex and too long, they become inefficient and can lose relevance. You cannot address complex challenges with a simple approach, nor should you try to apply holistic systems thinking to simple issues. "Everything should be made a simple as possible, but not simpler" (Albert Einstein).

This reinforces the point made earlier that we need to foster a paradoxical mindset of "this AND that" to optimize performance. We need a balance of turnover to bring in new knowledge and ideas while retaining the best of our existing experiences, ideas, and history of learning. Project-orientated organizations benefit from taking this highly interdependent approach to decision making with a balance of tactical survival responses that most align with strategic directions that consider both risks and benefits in a systems thinking[20] mode.

Knowledge, Projects, Context, and Sensemaking

Given the complexities highlighted so far, how do we make sense of the challenges and enable us to find the right direction, do the best projects, and transfer the appropriate knowledge to the right stakeholders? Sense-making is something that can be very different for different people. How we determine what is happening is a unique perception influenced by our own experiences, culture, and values. Why we believe something happens is a biased view of what we know and what we don't know. So even when we believe we know, it is just one person's view. When we share to discuss different perspectives, we are in a better position to "determine" what is real and what is not, but this is still not an absolute understanding. Collectively, we can get closer to what is happening, but we are still less able to determine why. As much as we would like to be able to "know for sure," reality is far less solid than we realize.

The real challenging question is how do we truly KNOW anything? In the modern era, there are people who just "Google it" to get THE answer. What they miss is this is just what one or many other people believe, and there are many other options if we look hard enough. Some "research" simply involves looking just hard and long enough to find the answer or solution we believe is or should be the right answer (which is very self-limiting). However, genuine search and discovery takes significant time and resources (which as highlighted earlier, people have less of now). Surveys consistently show a decreasing amount of genuine research involved in what is reported. This means more of what is reported across all forms of publication is based on provided content, which increasingly has not been fully challenged or validated by evidence-based review.

So as we start to understand that the world is more subjective than we were taught and we commence the journey toward knowing that we don't know, we can better determine how to act and why. We can make these actions more reliable by reflecting and challenging in interactive cycles to create value. Based on this balanced view of our subjective reality, we can better answer the question of what projects we should do and why?

What Do We Do When My Reality Does Not Match Your Perception?

Conflict is the most common reaction when knowledgeable professionals differ in opinion, mainly because professionals rely too heavily on their reality and experiences and are quick to reject other possible options. Rather than listen to other views and then debate them in order to learn, many people try to find ways to disprove the other perception. This human failing, often fueled by power and political games, can be the reason that many potentially valuable projects are rejected and many less-well-developed projects are supported. Knowing success is a lot more about understanding how to pitch an idea than the value of the idea. Knowing success is dependent on your ability to transfer sufficient knowledge in the appropriate language (usually finance) to convince the decision makers that your idea is better than the others they have heard recently. Of course, you then need to deliver that through your project implementation and passing the relevant knowledge to the stakeholder to deliver it, two forms of KNOWledge SUCCESSion often overlooked.

There are examples of forums where trusted knowledge flows freely between people across organizations to solve complex challenges and create mutual value. This is usually done for free and with no expectation of reciprocity. There is a strong sense of identity and belief in the value of sharing knowledge for the common good in voluntary communities, such as KM4dev, Melbourne KMLF, SIKM LEADERS, IKMS, ActKM, and the many product or service support forums. Often people contributing to these forums are doing so in their own time, so what drives them to do so? Such communities possess a strong sense of purpose driven by being appreciated and respected for being a catalyst to assist others perform better.

The concept of a knowledge catalyst worked very well during my involvement in a large international organization. The small knowledge team jokingly referred to themselves as the "corporate dating service." Many very significant projects generated measurable value across the organization (far more than the team cost, therefore generating solid return on investment). These projects would never have occurred without knowledge curators catalyzing connections and relationships. Their presence changed the dynamics, mindsets, focus, and flow of knowledge through the organization and how it was applied.

Imagine making a cake by just throwing the ingredients in and cooking without "informed mixing." When grandma makes it from experience, it is magnificent. Yet, when the inexperienced cook makes it following the recipe, it can be rather ordinary. Knowledge curation matters! Not because knowledge curators know or have a lot of "stuff" (content), but because they shift mindsets and connect people in ways that content, tools, and processes simply can't. Consider how much value you have received over the years from the interactions with people who provided you with a little inside knowledge or a perfectly timed anecdote that brought insights to change your direction or approach. The intimate environment of a well-led project has these moments of sharing on a daily basis and they trigger all the processes highlighted in Figure 1.3 in this forum (or others like it such as KM4 Dev or ActKM and the various local KM communities you interact with). Now imagine how much more difficult and less rewarding your role would be if no one every helped you with such insights. Organizations that have this (formally or informally) benefit enormously—whether they measure it or not. Leaders who leverage this will generate more sustainable performance (and these do exist if you look around at the top performers in some industries).

Knowledge is the fuel of success and social relationships are the lubricant for creative friction. Together, these combine to offer great potential for organizations. Important questions to ask yourself are: "Are you smart enough to act on this potential to realize the benefits through your projects? What do you do next to achieve this and why?"

Please join me throughout the rest of this book as we explore which options suit your contexts and how your KNOWledge SUCCESSion will lead to sustained improvement in personal and organizational performance.

Contributor Case Study

Dr. Vishnupriya Sengupta, Associate Director and Advisory Communications & Knowledge Lead, PwC India.

Disclaimer. The views expressed are those of the author and not necessarily that of the firm.

Spark Fires Global Connections and Knowledge Sharing

Imagine trying to connect, collaborate, and share content with people across a network of over 200,000 people in 157 countries. At PwC, one of the largest professional services firms in the world, aligning people to a common vision and combining knowledge and business strategies posed a serious challenge across the network.

Knowledge leaders across PwC often grappled with issues like:

- How can people and member firms effectively work together and share information?

- How do we connect people of similar experiences to interact around new ideas?
- How do we use content consistently across geographies?
- How do we transform our knowledge services?

As a solution, PwC first launched *Gateway*, a one-stop shop for knowledge comprising rich content from all the member firms. This worked to some extent, but it was not dynamic enough to keep pace with the digital times. The introduction of *Spark*, a new global real-time collaboration and networking tool on *Jive*, provided an opportunity to engage even better. It enabled us to interact in new ways, find people, share insights, discover information, and apply knowledge. Overnight, our knowledge changed from a transactional service to a transformational commodity that provided a great return on investment. The benefits of *Spark* were well received. PwC global knowledge leader, said, "With *Spark*, we now have a marketplace where people collaborate. It can get noisy and sometimes messy too, but it's alive and dynamic with people sharing knowledge."

Spark helps us connect seamlessly, collaborate effortlessly, and co-create innovatively. We can use the knowledge and expertise of the network to deliver better client value. We can connect with teammates and colleagues to work smarter and more dynamically. We can collect and share the views, opinions, and ideas of our people. PwC leaders across the network can also be empowered to connect and collaborate with their teams anytime, anyplace, and anywhere.

For instance, when one of the teams collectively produced a thought leadership document on *The Psychology of Incentives*, they wanted to share it with a wider audience. Rather than waiting for people to find the document, the team quickly increased awareness of it among internal target audiences by posting links in various interest groups. It went viral and effortlessly, the document and its concepts started being discussed and applied by many groups throughout the network, from PwC Canada to PwC Hong Kong in a way that was not previously possible.

In several instances, *Spark* has resulted in a reduction in the number of channels used, leading to dramatic improvements in communication, collaboration, and knowledge transfer across network teams. Connecting through *Spark* has helped increase visibility by allowing teams to form a community where one hadn't existed before. Teams are now unifying and learning faster than ever. PwC Switzerland and PwC Norway were using *Spark* as their intranet almost from day one, while other member firms have begun retiring their old systems and transitioning to *Spark*. PwC Japan made the move in 2013 and has seen its annual usage go up by 692 percent.

The rewards of *Spark* keep on giving. This year, PwC has for the 14th time been cited in the Global MAKE study for creating an environment for collaborative enterprise knowledge sharing. *Spark* is also a Gold award winner at the 2014 Intranet Innovation Awards and has been named a "Social, collaboration and communication" winner.

Today, there are 170,000 active members of *Spark*. Cross-border collaboration apart, *Spark* has accelerated the pace of executing deliverables and has taken the worry out of proposals. In short, *Spark* changed the way we work! In doing so, it has changed the perspective on how work is achieved and has improved our relationship with co-workers across dissolving borders.

Reflective Activities and Additional Learning Resources for the Curious Executive and or Students

Applying this learning in practice:

1. Ask the appropriate person if your organization has a comprehensive list of all projects with a link to your strategic plan. If this is available, ask how they were prioritized and if they are all fully resourced in the budget. If there is no list, challenge how you know if the right projects are being done.
2. Assess, ideally with a colleague, how much of your time is spent on routine tasks and how much is invested on change activities. Consider whether this ratio of time is adequate for you to remain competitive with the pace of change in your industry sector.

3. Look at the core knowledge you and your team possess and determine who else in the organization would benefit from knowing this. Find a way to engage with them to share the knowledge on a specific project or initiative so it can be shared in practice to save time rather than through a theoretical learning event that becomes extra time.

Additional learning resources:

www.intelligentanswers.com.au/KnowledgeSuccession

CHAPTER 2

Knowledge Co-Creation, Sustainability, and Adaptation

Executive Summary

This chapter describes why knowledge co-creation, sustainability, and adaptation are important interdependent factors that enable us to actively lead and manage projects. We explore why, how, and where these factors impact decision making as new knowledge emerges as the project progresses and flows through the organization. Key points of this chapter are:

- Continuous co-creation of knowledge is required for success because needs change in response to stakeholder desires and expectations, technological advances, and newly developed capabilities and ideas.
- Why knowledge needs to be recognized as a strategic asset, and how to "recycle" knowledge through continuous flows throughout the organization to create value and build capability.
- How to connect and leverage networks to accelerate the creation and flow of knowledge to sustain success over time.

Knowledge co-creation, sustainability, and adaptation benefit from:

1. Investing in knowledge as a strategic asset;
2. Understanding how knowledge drives innovation drives knowledge;
3. Knowing before others know to remain competitive; and
4. Doing knowledge projects for capability and learning.

Investing in Knowledge as a Strategic Asset

Whatcha gonna do with that duck?

We're surrounded by people who are busy getting their ducks in a row, waiting for the right moment.

Getting your ducks in a row is a fine thing to do. But deciding what you are going to do with that duck is a far more important issue.

—Seth Godin[1]

Many organizations have become obsessed with creating beautiful, glossy strategy documents full of amazing imagery. These documents are proudly thrust in your hand to impress you with how much important work the organization is "doing"—or at least planning to do. Where a well-thought-out strategy is broken down into aligned projects and implemented to generate synergies that pave a new path, there are successful outcomes. However, in many organizations, creating the strategy document is the completion of the work, and the ideas generated are not implemented to produce the desired results. This effectively takes the organization backward as the costs of creating ideas, planning, and documentation are incurred, but the benefits are not realized. Although this sounds ridiculous, it remains a common flaw, as was highlighted more than a decade ago by the insightful book *The Knowing Doing Gap*.[2] If anything, the "knowledge gap" between the strategic arm of the organization and the tactical one has widened. In our time of accelerating change, organizations have become more past and present oriented and less strategic. Successful organizations are ambidextrous,[3] in that they have creative people generating a range of options to achieve the organization's future vision AND have aligned implementation teams to prioritize these ideas into actionable projects that deliver the desired outputs and outcomes. That is, extending Godin's metaphor, these organizations think about which ducks are critical and why they are the priorities. They then invest in the resources and actions to ensure the ducks swim in harmony and reach their destinations, through tactics aligned with the overall direction.

One challenge in strategy creation is divergent in its thinking. Done well it looks forward to consider many options. However, strategy implementation is convergent: It looks to the shorter-term tasks with a view

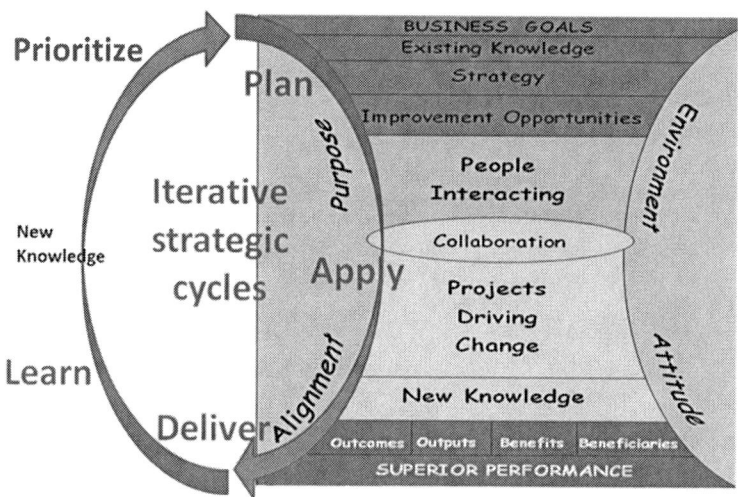

Figure 2.1 Knowledge-Flow Framework level 1: projects driving superior performance[4]

of getting them done. Too often, strategy creation and implementation are performed by people in separate silos of the organization, with different mindsets and decision-making styles. They simply do not connect or communicate with each other. The mindset and behaviors required to make strategic divergent decisions are almost the opposite of those required to coordinate the convergent actions of the implementers. Success requires an elevation of the conversations across multiple levels and the transfer of knowledge to ensure intent is understood and delivered. This is where experienced project leaders are at their most valuable. They can make the connections with both strategic outcomes and focus on tasks that most align with the longer-term benefit realization. Figures 2.1 and 2.2 highlight how central projects are to the delivery of organizational goals and the flow of knowledge between strategic plans and desired outcomes. In a modern business, projects are the way updated knowledge is embedded in the organization and, with good leadership, the mechanism through which new knowledge is created and ongoing learning happens.

Despite the long history of humans delivering large-scale projects, recognition of project management as a formal profession is a relatively recent phenomenon.[5] The basic task-oriented processes were developed by

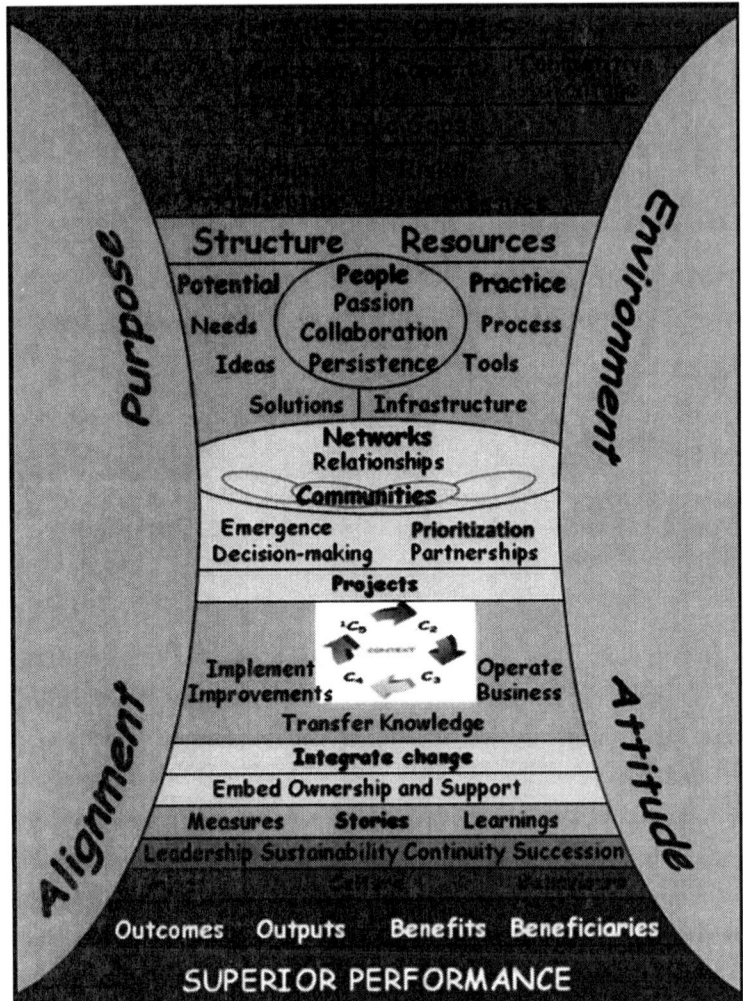

Figure 2.2 Knowledge-Flow Framework level 2: highlighting example influencing factors

Henry Gantt and Henri Fayol in the early 1900s, primarily in operational and logistical contexts. However, "formal recognition" of project management as a management field did not start until the mid-1960s. At that time, emerging project management associations started to define what projects are and how they should be done to deliver better outcomes. Since that time, huge progress has been made in the establishment of the "science" of WHAT projects are and HOW they can be done more efficiently and more effectively. However, most advances have focused on the processes and tactics within the project itself with little attention to the "WHY" project need to be done. As much "art" as science is involved in co-creating a new path through strategic projects. This exploration of where the organization is going, what it is becoming, and what soft skills capabilities it needs to get there are only recently starting to develop. Conducting business by project, rather than standard process, requires a whole new level of experience, expertise, and thinking focused on which projects before determining how to do them.

Success has come for leading organizations that balance project management with program leadership. Project professionals are now expected to go beyond processes and reporting to enhance the human aspects of delivering effective projects. This is correcting one of the biggest limitations of projectization. That is, looking beyond a short-term independent perspective measured within the project to an assessment of the project's continued achievement: A shift from tangible outputs within the timeframe of the project to include the intangible outcomes from the project beyond completion. Isolating a project makes it easier to measure and control, but it disconnects the project from the main thrust of the operation of the organization. If this disconnect persists for too long, the project's relevance reduces and the main decision makers and stakeholders can lose sight of this in the wider operational organization. Projects are more influential and value generating when maintained in close alignment with the evolving business, where they can be adjusted as an agile solution. Thus, projects remain a vital piece in a larger and more complex mix of people, capability, and knowledge in the evolving organizational and social context.

The project management literature, both academic and practical, has a wide range of definitions for a project. Although most are reasonably well aligned, it is beneficial to be aware of these differences and which aspects of projects are valued in your immediate context. While there are too many differences to attempt a detailed discussion here, the more respected thought leaders collectively highlight general characteristics of projects. A key insight is to differentiate projects from "normal" or routine work. Projects are considered temporary initiatives and involve a discrete set of tasks designed and implemented to bring about change and new value. That is, in simplistic terms, successful projects enable us to change the ways things are done for the better. This enhanced way, system, process, structure, relationship, etcetera becomes embedded into a new "normal way of doing things" until the next project continues the cycle of evolution. Projectized organizations have blurred this boundary, and in some matrix organizations the "normal way of doing things" is constant change through new projects. Without strategic alignment of the parallel projects and knowledge sharing between them, this can lead to disaster. However, when well planned and implemented, this approach can generate sustained competitive advantage; especially important in areas of rapid innovation such as the technology sector.

PMI's *Project Management Body Of Knowledge*[6] is one of the most respected and commonly used guides to help project managers understand the terminology and scope of processes and activities to become a competent project manager. It highlights the traditional "Iron Triangle" criteria to be managed, time, quality, cost (resources), and scope, and invests considerable detail on these and related tangible factors. However, attaining the next level of understanding to effectively lead or manage a project requires awareness well beyond the 400 plus the PM BOK pages. Success is accelerated through applying subjective emotional intelligence to supplement the largely rational ideas. Project management professional associations such as AIPM and PMI (and their equivalents in other countries) started to form from the mid-1960s to promote the more holistic development of project professionals. They provide connections for inexperienced people joining the field to ask questions, seek mentors, and develop networks of trusted allies to support ongoing career development. The International Project Management Association formed in Europe in 1967 to assist the development of the project management profession by (1) enabling the sharing of ideas, (2) stimulating forums for dialogue and knowledge development, (3) creating of standards and guidelines, (4) providing a political body for advising of policy and governance, (5) sponsoring development research, and (6) providing education and training for new people to the field.[7] This supports development of project professionals with a wider set of knowledge, capabilities, and experiences beyond textbook knowledge. The tacit dimensions of experience to foster a social fabric laced with intangible insights make the profession more productive and able to innovate more effectively. The challenge is how do we embed this same thinking into the individual project environment so that it becomes part of the overall fabric of the organization rather than being an isolated island?

The Project (or Program) Management Office (PMO) has evolved into a role in some highly professional organizations where a portfolio approach is being adopted to align projects into a program of strategic initiatives with shared resources and common processes.[8,9] That said, establishing a successful PMO is a complex project in itself and has been a significant challenge for many organizations, resulting in some miserable failures. Adding a layer of strategic leadership over the PMO management process will increase success, reduce risks, and enhance overall performance.[10]

A key insight from this section is that projects generate new knowledge and that both tacit and explicit knowledge are required to accelerate the success of projects. The relationship between knowledge, capability, learning, and performance does not happen by accident; it requires strategic leadership and deliberate attention to align the cycles, as discussed in later sections of this chapter (Figure 2.2).

Understanding How Knowledge Drives Innovation Drives Knowledge

You can know the best way to approach a challenge or have a great new idea, but to get it done usually requires the support of others. As Johann Wolfgang von Goethe stated:

Knowing is not enough, we must apply. Willing is not enough, we must do.

The world is littered with good ideas that never reached completion, or even grew beyond being just an idea. While the majority smugly protects the little idea they plan to someday implement to perfection, the modern entrepreneur quickly develops and tests the idea to failure or fruition, learning in the process and creating new insights and knowledge. Getting support for your idea can help make it more robust and expand it into something greater and more attractive for development. However, securing support can be the biggest barrier for many projects, especially securing support of senior decision makers or external investors. Organizations often have many potential projects that simply never get implemented or good ideas that were badly implemented and failed. Effectively pitching your project idea to the relevant decision makers is an important part of being a successful manager and even more critical for leaders.

Humans have highly evolved decision-making mechanisms, which are heavily influenced by immediate emotional and social impact. Knowing how this largely subconscious process works influences how you lead others to make a decision in your favor. Your role is to lead them toward your option and engage them emotionally so they rationalize positively about your proposal. If your target stakeholder's first impression is positive, they will seek reasons to support your idea. However, if their immediate feeling is one of dislike or discomfort, they will search for reasons to reject the idea.[11] When pitching your idea to others, it is critical you hit on an emotional tag they care about very quickly, so that the immediate reaction is to embrace the idea to subsequently secure rational support. Tell people what they need to do and you are likely to be rejected; engage people in why your idea or initiative is good for them, and hopefully others, and you are more likely to get what you ask for. Be warned: There is a fine line between influence for mutual benefit and manipulation of others for your own benefit at their expense. Ethics, fair play, and perceptions of value all play a critical role when pitching your message and the benefits claimed.

Every successful project leader understands the importance of influence. They also benefit from understanding the different ways in which people come to know what they need to do. This is rarely as clear-cut as one may think, as initial reactions, and therefore final outcomes, are more dependent on perceptions than facts. One amazing example of how one small misperception can completely change everything is the case of Taylor and Sons.[12] Beginning in 1875, this Welsh family business had operated for five generations and was considered credible and successful at delivering significant projects. An office of the British Government made a spelling error in the name of another company, leading suppliers and customers to believe Taylor and Sons Ltd was in liquidation. This false understanding from a usually reliable source completely disrupted the previously healthy company's strategic partnerships and caused its rapid demise and eventual closure. It cost the British Government millions of pounds and is testimony to the power of perception over fact.

This is why trusted relationships and resilience can be more important than robustness of your evidence. Sometimes, it does not matter how good your idea is: Your ability to create the right perception can override all the facts you provide. Unfortunately, some people understand this very well and manipulate the "facts" to make a project look much better than it is in reality. So the opposite effect is also possible. That is, ideas that were never going to be feasible are invested in, based on poorly collated or deliberately compromised data, and the project subsequently fails. The relationship between facts and perception and their impact on reality and outcomes is one that benefits from robust challenges and multiple voices early in the development stages.

The argument for knowledge-based decision making is not new. In the 4th Century BCE, Aristotle's *Rhetoric* described three modes of persuasion: (1) ethos (ethics and credibility), (2) pathos (emotional and symbolic perceptions), and (3) logos (logic and rationale). Aristotle argued that each one can be used to persuade an audience and the three combined are powerful. A powerful approach starts with pathos to engage an audience emotionally, then uses ethos to build credibility, and finishes with the rationale of logos. Aristotle also acknowledged that these can be inappropriately used to manipulate or misguide by reducing the facts and emphasizing the emotional aspects. Ever since, these factors have been deliberately used by a wide range of people to secure what they want, from ethical social developers, to advertisers to confidence tricksters. See deeper discussion on this in Chapter 12 for stakeholder engagement.

Although personal preferences, pet projects, position, and politics all play a role in how projects are prioritized, you secure kudos when you demonstrate your project is aligned with the organization's goals and is likely to deliver benefits with diminished risk. Like much of the advice in this book, this seems obvious. Remarkably, many eager idea creators and project managers cannot answer this basic return on investment question in one sentence when asked. For some people, the interdependent operational cogs that drive the aspirations of business strategy to generate organizational outcomes are a complex, indecipherable mess. However, when viewed from a high-level knowledge-flow perspective, the value of any specific idea, project, or program can be assessed within the context of that organization. Figure 2.1 shows the cycles of knowledge and energy flows that will ensure projects deliver the desired outputs and outcomes for the organization.

Figure 2.1 represents a simple view of the flow of knowledge through the organization from the top-level strategy, through to the bottom line. Knowledge of the organization's capabilities and vision are required to guide strategy—although as stated earlier, too often, strategy teams work in isolation of the knowledge bank in the organization. Superior performance is measured as the delivery of desired tangible outputs and sustainable intangible outcomes, with aligned projects being the engine that drives the actions required to connect strategy to actions. Starting at this level provides the ability to see the "Bigger Picture" and overall flow of knowledge through the iterative strategic cycles. Once this is understood, conversations delve into each of the higher-level components to ensure that subcomponents are in place to keep the flow in the right direction and at the right pace. Some, but not all, example considerations of the next-level subcomponents are shown in Figure 2.2. Another cycle of conversation can go below this to assess what tools and process changes may be necessary to make each of these components connect smoothly and efficiently. Organizations that successfully manage these flows—creating optimal paths and removing barriers—generate new knowledge and stimulate relationships and learning in a positive environment. This in turn accelerates success and builds stronger foundation for future sustained performance as the cycles progress.

Knowledge and personal experiences are used throughout the organization to support decision making and maintain the flow throughout the cycle and into the next iteration. Iterations can range from moments in informal conversations to verify progress, through to project milestone reviews or on annual financial cycle basis.

The Knowledge-Flow Framework can act as a simple conversation stimulant to highlight the complexity of components considered and to enable a range of perspectives about their impact to be included. Some organizations have great strength in the upper part of the flow, and are good at creating and defining strategy. But without complementary strengths in the bottom half to connect and implement the strategy, these organizations fail to deliver. They may be overly optimistic or poor at prioritization, and therefore spread resources too thin to deliver anything well. Others can be too focused on the future and not implement the projects needed in the immediate cycle to be ready for their envisioned future. Other organizations have strengths in the lower half of the Knowledge-Flow Framework. Typically, they are excellent at implementing projects, but less competent at understanding which are the best projects to complete to remain viable and competitive. Some are more past focused, and so keep recycling outdated knowledge and maintaining capabilities less relevant to future performance. To enable knowledge flow, key people must be engaged in conversations that connect the two areas of the organization. The framework can be used to stimulate discussions on strengths and weakness and barriers and how to balance the flow. These conversations highlight how to keep the co-creation of new knowledge and the cycling of existing knowledge at the pace required to achieve ongoing sustained performance. Aligning these cycles with the organizational goals helps the organization evolve and build an inclusive environment. In doing so, projects become better aligned, teams less frustrated, better informed, and prepared, and resources more effectively allocated. This increases trust and provides greater harmony. None of these largely intangible outcomes is easy to measure, but all are more important that many of the tangible measures. Einstein was credited as stating (though the originator is probably William Cameron a quarter of a century earlier, highlighting that "new knowledge" is often an adaptation or adoption of earlier insights):

> *Not everything that counts can be counted and not everything that can be counted counts.*

Focusing effort on any single part of the Knowledge-Flow Framework, without consideration of the other parts, will not work as well as desired. Siloed organizations become inefficient because the flow of knowledge becomes laminar rather than turbulent. Creativity and innovation are stimulated when knowledge is shared and remixed through an adaptive co-creation of new insights.[13] Creating siloed disconnected organizations is like deciding to build a human body piece by piece rather than as a unit. For example, constructing the heart or the brain in isolation and then building the other organs is not workable as none can operate alone. They coexist in complex interdependence. Organizational knowledge flow is similar, in that it requires a coordinated effort to get the system to work as a whole. This IS difficult, complex, and emergent and why many people do not understand what is not working and why. The concept of holistic or systems thinking[14] is not new, it is just not widely practiced. It is surprising how little effort is invested in facilitating this cross-disciplinary interaction and how siloed many organizations have become, despite insights on achieving this interaction in the project management literature.[15]

The essence of the Knowledge-Flow Framework (Figure 2.2) is that stimulating strategic knowledge co-creation and cyclic knowledge flows accelerates business performance. To highlight this, the next four paragraphs illustrate how knowledge flows through the framework and how these components are interconnected. Note that the first two paragraphs highlight activities that lead toward the creation and prioritization of aligned projects (upper portion and then center of the framework). The third covers the aspects that happen during and after the implementation of projects to integrate the changes and realize the value promised (middle to bottom of the framework). The fourth paragraph discusses the flow from inputs to outputs and how they connect the new knowledge and learning back to the next cycle to inform future directions and strategy formation. While not all the possible connections can be covered in one short description of the flow, those highlighted through this level 2 pass of the framework show just how connected these aspects need to be. Removing any part of these connections creates a barrier that effectively blocks the flow and damages performance.

Superior performance requires starting with business goals that are within the capabilities and capacity of the organization, and having sufficient knowledge to understand what the organization's competitive advantages are. This knowledge drives the focus areas of the organization's strategy and highlights gaps that could lead to weaknesses and opportunities. In addressing the strategic opportunities, issues, and risks, the organization needs to mobilize people and other resources around ideas and concepts that offer potential for improvement when put into action. There are not usually sufficient resources to put all possible ideas and concepts into practice. So prioritization enables only the most valuable concepts to be developed into projects. It is more beneficial to focus resources and capabilities on fewer projects that offer the biggest return on investment to implement them well, than to implement everything and end up doing all poorly.

Choosing which ideas offer the biggest benefits works best when discussed with the resident experts in the field, accompanied by peers from associated fields. This enables diverse views to be explored and emergent ideas to be generated. Without open "conversations that matter" and engaging the diversity of opinions and perspectives, unforeseen opportunities are less likely to arise and innovation becomes stifled. Within communities of practice, knowledge, views, and opinions on issues and opportunities are exchanged and form the foundation concepts for projects. Sharing concepts between communities, through the associated networks, highlights other possibilities around the concepts and enhances their scope of application. Outputs from the conversations are project proposals, aligned with business strategy. The projects are reviewed considering both tangible outputs and intangible outcomes.

Once the optimal projects are approved as an aligned program, they need to be implemented in a way that optimizes success. Disciplined project management processes, which incorporate knowledge principles and iterative value challenge cycles,[16] enable the projects to be completed effectively and potential benefits to be realized. When these activities are performed in an aligned manner and with a shared purpose, superior performance is almost inevitable. The combined process and knowledge flow provides a positive spiral of experiential learning, which builds the capabilities of individuals, teams, and the organization as a whole.

It is not enough for a leader to describe the outcomes, outputs, and benefits generically, especially in the absence of understanding the resources, capabilities, and knowledge required to achieve these. Provisions of time and effort for the input side is critical. Without this, all efforts invested may be wasted. Competent leaders understand that they benefit from engaging others' perspectives through conversations about the input side of the equation to collectively list and prioritize the specifics of the program. Leaders benefit from asking questions and fostering the environment where the best options can emerge from the interested parties. The framework connects a mixture of key elements, process, and relationships to form a knowledge-informed connection between strategy and implementation. This simplifies the way in which the leader can leverage what is known, what needs to be known, and what is being learned through each cycle. This helps to maintain focus on what is delivering value and to keep performance aligned with business goals. Enhancing performance through the better use of knowledge assets is the ultimate achievement of high-performing organizations. This is why good organizations invest in a PMO and a dedicated knowledge support team. Of course, these investments need to work well and become self-supporting to justify their existence. Leaders who observe business-aligned benefits continuously flowing from a PMO or knowledge program, which addresses strategic gaps, increases capabilities, and builds competitive advantage, are going to ensure it remains well resourced. Awareness of the performance of the program delivers self-sustainability, just as lack of awareness can cause its demise.

If leaders are not aware of how PMOs or knowledge teams pay for themselves, why would they want to maintain them? This is why the framework starts with goals and ends with performance, but in the middle focuses on specific projects with specific outcomes and benefits. Without something specific to focus on and collaborate around, knowledge sharing itself does not necessarily add tangible benefits. It works best when targeted around specific projects and initiatives because benefits are more easily seen by those involved. However, unstructured knowledge flows can also add intangible benefits as these stimulate trust and relationship development. Such connections help to align stakeholder support for critical projects, so should not be discounted. Although hard to assess, these intangible aspects of projects should be acknowledged as important to strategy development and encouraged. However, without tangible benefits regularly flowing, such programs lose momentum or go underground into informal networks. These informal networks are important for performance, but convincing senior executives of their "real worth" can be difficult if they, and the value they create, are not visible.

Another advantage of the framework is it can be used as a communications and engagement tool. Potential sponsors and participants who are not initially prepared to invest the time to fully understand the program of projects can see the potential from this diagram. It is easy to grasp and it helps stakeholders see why one project is a priority and another is a vaguely interesting curiosity. The flow and interrelationships between the elements of the framework become more obvious and removed from the detail of individual projects. The process is generic, but the specifics of your projects, your focus areas, and your balance of short-term and long-term benefits make it applicable to your context. The conversations stimulated by this tool differ in organizations depending on the organizational culture and context, and the level of support. When sufficient supporters participate in such constructive dialogues, they create a well-aligned program of strategic initiatives.

Knowing Before Others Know to Remain Competitive

We have been discussing why projects are the ideal way to implement positive change in organizations and how this improves performance and drives innovation. However, many projects fail to deliver their expected outcomes, and project failure has a significant negative economic impact across a wide range of industries.[17] A variety of sophisticated project management methods and tools for project activities including planning, budget control, and risk and resource management have been developed to increase project success rates. So far, these management tools have not sufficiently evolved as effective techniques to manage team behaviors and dynamics, or to determine which projects will be best. Over the past decade, a growing body of academic literature has focused on these soft skill aspects of projects, including social, political, learning, value generation, and professional development. This shift in emphasis from doing the mechanical tasks of individual projects to viewing projects as steps in a longer-term series of development activities is significant. While a project is delivered as specific piece of work, there is also value in understanding the social and knowledge elements evolving from that project. The ability to recycle these new capabilities and behaviors into the next projects and phases is a major step toward more sustainable performance over time. This approach also recognizes the environment projects operate in as an important factor in the development of the project management profession.

Another factor contributing to this evolution of the discipline is the increasing tendency for professionals to view their own lives as a series of mini projects instead of a traditional career within a few organizations.

This has advantages and disadvantages. The thinking helps to understand that projects are not just temporary objects to be completed and forgotten, as every job develops one's capabilities to secure the next role. Each project for an organization develops the capabilities and knowledge to evolve the organization. Conversely, as project managers see themselves as a highly mobile resource, they move more frequently on to other projects in other organizations and industries. This results in a constant hemorrhage of knowledge for the organization, often at the worst times possible, just as the project handover is taking place. It is difficult for organizations to build up "Deep Smarts,"[18] when expertise departs before being transferred to others in the organization for ongoing operations of project delivery. This loss is further complicated by the fact that the best performers with the best knowledge and relationships skills (termed Multipliers[19]) are most sought after and move the most, accelerating the losses. The growth of social media sites such as LinkedIn and Facebook has enabled people to build their personal networks independent of their employer and has also exacerbated the challenge of retaining knowledge. Keeping critical knowledge is now a significant challenge for most organizations and this challenge is likely to increase.

So when you are losing your good performers and knowledge at a great rate, how can you remain competitive? The good news is organizations are on an equal playing field, so your competitors have the same issues. However, the balance of power has now shifted more toward the employees. They have much more choice about where they want to work and can be more easily found by competing organizations. As an individual this is a positive shift for you, but as a team leader and project manager it can make things more complicated and increase the risks of failure.

Luck can be a good thing, but is not a solid foundation for strategy! Quickly taking advantage of lucky opportunities when they emerge can generate value and should be leveraged in harmony with a robust portfolio of projects, but not relied upon as a foundation of your strategy. Serendipity can create benefits if you have an adaptable mindset and are able to see potential that was not intended, although this is not a common skill as people are often too patterned in their thinking to notice the value in unintended outcomes. Too often things that were not planned for are seen as problems. Some are genuine issues and should be dealt with appropriately. Theoretically, these can be preemptively avoided or limited with proper due diligence and risk-mitigation actions, but unpredictable challenges arise. Knowledge loss at the end of projects is a good example of a likely problem that can be seen as an opportunity with the right mindset. Knowledge loss hurts organizations severely and yet so few of them act to minimize it. Organizations that are less challenged by this issue are those that look more holistically at the problem and treat it as an opportunity. They create an environment where people feel comfortable, safe, and involved to build identity, loyalty, and participation. Naturalistic or environmental themes have been used by a number of writers when describing how learning organizations[20] work and evolve.

When leaders make the effort to be well informed from both internal knowledge flows and external insights, they are aware of looming changes and act on them before they are forced. Their proactive insights help them to understand the long-term implications of their decisions and ensure the organization is future-focused and operates in a self-sustaining manner. They remain innovators in the business world, ahead of the game and ultimately market leaders, because they are outcome and development focused as much as output focused.[21]

A related philosophical perspective of this approach is how knowledge is valued. A scarcity approach—knowledge is power—can provide a consultant with some short-term, high-priced transactions on their knowledge to provide a few with a perceived competitive advantage. However, a growing movement supports the principle of abundance, which makes knowledge more freely available to ensure the maximum value can be shared by many.

__Knowledge is Power__ to a politician who wants to control access to resources and opportunities, but to a well-informed leader __knowledge is powerful when shared, socialized and collaboratively acted on!__

The advent of free social media tools has enabled greater sharing of information and knowledge across traditional boundaries of time, geography, and organizational firewalls. This creates a different business model, built more around relationships than content. Some consultants now freely provide their ideas and concepts to anyone who wants them, provided their source is acknowledged. This increases the awareness and scope of application of their ideas, which they can learn from, and enhances their reputation as a provider of value. They can generate revenue from working with clients to apply the ideas more effectively, rather than charge them for bland content. Crowdsourcing[22] is a good example of how the innovation game is changing because of this way of thinking.

In this environment, employees collaborate and feel part of something bigger than just work. Career opportunities are flexible and often tailored to individual's strengths. Employees continuously build their capabilities through experiential learning opportunities and by participating in both colocated projects and virtual interactions.

If you want to retain your individual, team, and organizational knowledge, build your capabilities, and lead the innovation across your industry, adopt a mindful approach toward environmental evangelism! Doing this will attract and retain the best people. Show them there is a continuous stream of strategically aligned projects through which they will be challenged, valued, and in which they will generate meaningful trusted relationships. Those who do this best reap what they sow and, perhaps not surprisingly, more often have the best ideas for the next big thing.

Doing Knowledge Projects for Capability and Learning

As the pace of technology development has accelerated and the scope and reach of organizations have increased, larger-scale projects have become more common with greater value at stake and greater knowledge transfer challenges. Although these changes create potential for greater value creation, they also introduce increased complexity, higher risks, and more stakeholders to influence and transfer knowledge to. The simplest form of projects can still be done by an individual in a short time by themselves, but in most modern business contexts an average project is significantly more involved, and requires a team of people, a significant budget, and considerable time. To smart organizations, this is an investment in future capability. The knowledge developed before, during, and after the implementation of the project is seen as a significant asset to be leveraged in future.

Projects are defined in different ways by a vast range of texts, most of which focus on the process of delivering the project, with little attention on the project as a learning and development event for the individuals involved and the organization as a whole. A search for "project management" on Amazon.com in 2013 produced 65,000 titles to browse. When repeated in January 2015, this same search produced an increased output of 98,800 titles. Despite the increasing volumes written on this topic in recent times, limited literature exists on proactively aligning projects to increase the knowledge foundations of the organization. Science research has traditionally done this better, with a competitive collaboration approach working quite well over time. Each scientist collaborates in the race to "discover" new things and contribute to the body of knowledge. In doing so, they leverage each other's knowledge through publications as projects progress. More recently, this cycle has been disrupted as commercial influences are making discoveries less openly available. Some commercial organizations have a similar approach in how they perform their internal product and service development to leapfrog the latest releases of their competitors. This involves a different sort of knowledge transfer by remaining in touch with what others are doing and the consumer response to this, to inform your own development projects. This approach enables rapid improvement or evolution through larger knowledge foundations driving cycles of incremental or disruptive innovation.

The project management literature is largely separated from the literature on knowledge management, change management, leadership, and innovation. However, these are all closely linked. Each of these disciplines has significant overlaps, and decisions made in one could greatly impact the others across disciplines. Figure 2.3 highlights the benefits that could be achieved if more cross-discipline adaptation of ideas took place. It suggests that overall performance is a balance of integrating each of these areas to enable a flow of knowledge informed by them all. The first instance is to create strategic projects to change organizations, then subsequently to adaptively generate a flow of knowledge-informed actions that supports effective implementation of these projects. In doing so, they co-create new knowledge, build capabilities, and stimulate learning. Repeated iterations for these cycles increase performance and competitive advantage.

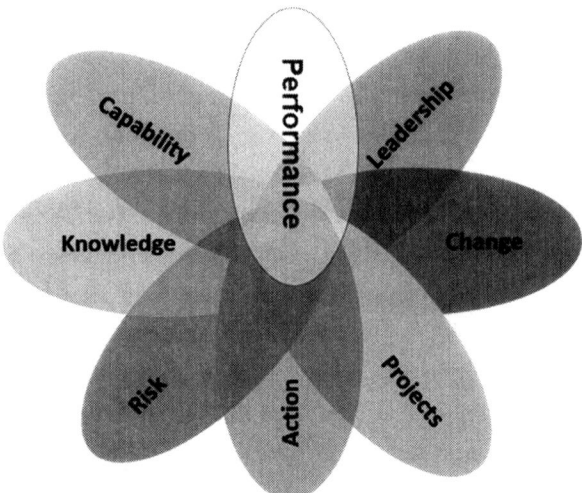

Figure 2.3 The Performance flower, synchronized cycles of knowledge creation, and application

Contributor Case Study

Vincent Ribiere, Founder Institute for Knowledge and Innovation, SE Asia

IKISEA Cross-Pollination of Knowledge Communities

The Institute for Knowledge and Innovation (IKI) was founded at the George Washington University in 2001 by Dr. Michael Stankosky (Professor at the Engineering Management and Systems Engineering (EMSE) Department) and Dr. William Halal (Business School). At the time, the George Washington University was the first university in the United States to offer a Master's degree and Doctorate of Science in the new emerging field of Knowledge Management. Feel free to visit the I2KI Web site to learn more about our parent institute. Vincent Ribiere completed his PhD as part of this program, and thought there was value in establishing a branch of the IKI into Asia. He had a passion to continue the work of Dr. Stankosky to expand the reach of postgraduate learning about knowledge and innovation.

In 2007, Dr. Vincent Ribiere (Director for Asian Activities at IKI) moved to Thailand and with the help of Dr. Lugkana Worasinchai and of Dr. Aurilla Aurélie Bechina Arntzen founded the South-East Asian Branch of IKI (IKI-SEA). In 2009, a Memorandum of Understanding (MOU) was signed between the IKI of the George Washington University and the South–East Asian branch of IKI (IKI-SEA) hosted by Bangkok University in Bangkok, Thailand. IKI-SEA now runs a vibrant PhD program in the area of knowledge and innovation with their first students graduating in 2014.

Reflective Activities and Additional Learning Resources for the Curious Executive and Students

Applying this learning in practice:

1. List the critical (cannot buy) knowledge in your organization and where it is held. Consider the consequences to the organization if this is lost (especially to your competitors). Discuss what actions you are taking to mitigate against this risk.
2. Use the image in Figure 2.2 to highlight where your knowledge-flow strengths and weaknesses are. Compare your perspectives on this to others in a workshop. Consider how to remove the barriers to knowledge flow and enhance the aspects that are stimulating flow and co-creation.
3. Use the Knowledge Flower (Figure 2.3) to challenge what parts of your performance are underperforming. Think how this is related to knowledge flows (or a lack thereof). How can you operate differently to change this and increase performance?

Additional learning resources:
www.intelligentanswers.com.au/KnowledgeSuccession

CHAPTER 3

Projects as Vehicles of Change and Knowledge Transfer

Executive Summary

Chapter 3 challenges readers to determine if their organization is sufficiently mature and connected to optimize knowledge flows and ensure value creation is aligned with their organization's business direction. Key points of this chapter are:

- Do you know who your knowledge brokers are and their core expertise?
- Who or what blocks the flow of knowledge and what are they risking?
- Is knowledge being proactively and effectively co-created, transferred, and applied between development projects and the ongoing business processes?

Key questions to ask to uncover your readiness to leverage projects as vehicles of change:

1. Is your organization knowledge ready for the future?
2. Do you have appropriate mechanisms for knowledge co-creation and transfer?
3. How do you monitor knowledge adoption and effective application?

Because this chapter is about the future, it is more about asking you questions than providing answers. This is because, assuming you want to be successful in leading others rather than following, only you can create your own future as a leader. To do that you have to find answers to critical questions others cannot answer, or find better answers, or find answers more quickly in order to lead. Failing to do this relegates you to a follower, at least until you can become a leader should you invest the emotional, social, and rational intelligence and the effort to bring these to fruition. The book title *Questions Are the Answer*[1] is a very provocative piece of reflective advice. So ask yourself: *Am I asking the right questions and finding a range of suitable options and then prioritizing these into the best possible actions and implementing these through well-executed projects?* If you can honestly say yes and provide evidence you are doing this sustainably, consistently, efficiently, and effectively, you are probably a leader already or well on the way to becoming one. Leave out any of the words in the prior two sentences and you are probably not a leader, unless you have been very lucky. Luck should be taken advantage of when it comes your way, but it does not form the basis of a robust strategy.

Is Your Organization Knowledge Ready for the Future?

Everyone dreams about what their future might hold. It provides inspiration and a sense of identity and challenge. People who do not have dreams are less content with their lives and people who dream well beyond their realistic capabilities and resources become frustrated. An effective dream should be just beyond your current capability and capacity to deliver so that it lifts your spirit and motives you to move toward it. However, it remains a dream until you commit to act in a way that will take you toward delivery. We all know someone who is forever saying, "*One day I will …*"; however, they will never get there because they have not actually considered what it takes to deliver the dream, started to build the resources to make it possible, or made the required effort to realize it. A dream is a good start to preparing for the future, but it is just one step of many.

It is important to understand that the dream of keeping everything exactly as it is now, soon turns into a nightmare of irrelevance as the rest of the world whooshes past.

In 2015 the Information and Knowledge Management Society (iKMS. org) of Singapore announced their Knowledge Ready Organization

(KRO) Awards. These awards are aimed to encourage organizations to proactively create strategic initiatives to make them future-ready through the development of knowledge and capabilities. KRO awards highlight the benefits of a forward-looking mindset by recognizing "organizations that lead, strategize, implement and measure knowledge systems, processes and practices to remain competitive." History is cluttered with the debris of organizations that were once leaders in their fields and thought they would always be the best. Overconfidence eventually reduces them to "other miscellaneous brand" in the balance sheet. Continuous improvement helps organizations to remain efficient, but with rapid changes in technology and consumer expectations, some disruptive innovation is also necessary. Edward de Bono summed it up nicely in his phrase, "EBNE—Excellent, But NOT Enough."

Remaining among the top performers requires significant adaptation and adoption over time and progressing more rapidly and successfully than your competition. These changes are usually achieved through a program of aligned projects. The iKMS KRO assessment criteria have been designed to increase the chances of remaining in a state of readiness in a complex and uncertain world, through building a combination of robustness and resilience. The KRO criteria are: Strategy, Leadership, Culture, Process, Technology, and Impact. What I like about these awards is that they connect the interdependent future-focused aspects of organizations and demonstrate the synergies and impact these have in terms of value and sustainability. Deliberate effort is made to explore what the future might hold and what needs to be done in order to perform well in the new states that emerge. This includes the acceptance that these criteria themselves will change over time.

The Baldridge award offers another example of an award that supports organizations to constantly evolve. This award was created from the philosophies of the quality movement in the late 1980s and has been internationally recognized. It provides a solid framework of criteria that enhance organizational sustainability and performance. Their purpose is to embed quality across the organization to enhance competitiveness. This increases awareness and investment in building new capabilities, facilitating communication, and sharing across organizations and as a guide for benchmarking and learning. The assessment criteria include ever-improving results in value creation for consumers and stakeholders, organizational effectiveness, and learning at both individual and organizational levels. The hidden insight is that this focus of attention on achieving the intangibles brings about the tangible benefits, not the other way round. Too often "Balanced-Scorecard" approaches focus too heavily on the tangibles and miss the intangible aspects, which are hard to measure and even harder to achieve. Attention to how well you achieved past activities does not assure your future. It is better to blend in assessments of important subjective aspects of organizational relationships, even though these cannot be accurately measured. These things will determine future success. Past experiences and performances do help, but every sports person knows that fame only lasts until your next event. Plenty of others out there are trying to displace you from the top.

The Australian Business Excellence Framework[2] provides a set of integrated aspects to generate future-readiness. SAI Global connects similar characteristics of leadership strategy, soft skills, and operational procedures in a flow of knowledge through organizations over time. These are a few examples of the many business excellence awards and frameworks available, often with government support. Simply search the Internet for "Business Excellence Framework" and a plethora of options is returned. Each framework has its own processes, graphics, and assessment criteria. MAKE Awards (Most Admired Knowledge Enterprise), a range of innovation and creativity awards and benchmarking studies from organizations like APQC (American Productivity and Quality Center, APQC.org), has a mantra of Explore, Measure, Network to highlight the value of mixing discovery and social connection to build readiness. Organizations such as PMI (Project Management Institute, PMI.org) provide a wealth of opportunities to build your knowledge and grow your career. Only recent editions of the *PMI Book of Knowledge* have started to include insights on soft skills development. Each industry and sector has something to draw upon. These resources provide a rich vein of ideas that can be mined for nuggets of insight to bring into your future-ready deliberations.

The key to gaining success from these awards and resources is not from winning the award or simply collecting the knowledge. Success comes from adapting the insights into your own practices—personally and professionally and across the organization. Acquiring knowledge and winning awards do help with awareness of the program and its benefits. However, achieving genuine future-readiness requires considerable effort in applying the ideas widely and consistently. The real benefits of awards and frameworks are they provide an object around which to engage people in "Conversations That Matter" about how to best progress toward THEIR future. Organizations with this mindset and culture know what their priorities are and why. They know how what they do today fits into the strategy and how it moves them toward the organization's goals. They know who they need to interact with to achieve this in the most effective and efficient way. Most importantly, they know how to unlearn things that they may have been good at and enjoyed, but are now irrelevant for future success. If the focus is on winning an award, the level of benefit is reduced. However, when the award focuses and aligns efforts to optimal actions and continuous improvement, success and benefits flow. Achieving an award becomes just another positive outcome on the path toward future-readiness.

This demonstrates that there are many credible and reliable resources on how to prepare for the future. Despite the availability of such resources, organizational failure continues to be common. When there is no shortage of good-quality advice, why are so many organizations so poorly prepared for the future? Prior to 1965, the average lifespan of organizations listed on Standard and Poor's S&P 500 was consistently in excess of 30 years. By 2015, this lifespan had reduced to barely 20 years.[3] The S&P 500 has increasingly shown significant churn with previously larger-than-life organizations disappearing and new ones appearing. In 2010–11, iconic companies including Eastman Kodak, RadioShack, and *The New York Times* were removed from the S&P 500 Index. Since the early 2000s, a bundle of new technology-based organizations have appeared in the S&P 500, including Google, E*TRADE, eBay, Juniper Networks, Amazon, Comcast, and Netflix. What the world wants and how we get it is constantly changing. Those organizations aware of this see this change as opportunity; those that do not remain vigilant disappear.

Successful companies are often lulled into complacency by how well their business models have been—and indeed still are—working. But just because your current model is widely used and profitable doesn't mean it will serve you well in the future.[4]

The fact that that many organizations set next year's budget based on last year's performance, plus or minus inflation and percentage, demonstrates the inadequacy of this past-focused mindset. This action asserts that our past is the key piece of knowledge we need to determine our future. However, some projects and routine processes may no longer be relevant. More importantly, activities yet to done, which will become the future activities of the organization, are not part of that equation. How can these be simply budgeted for against what has been done previously? Allocating resources focusing on the past is like driving to work looking only at the rearview mirror instead of out the front window. Genuine future planning requires insights from your best people across all levels of the organization, to first determine where the value will be. These people need to identify what to reinvent and why to collectively determine how that potential value is best secured. This requires a well-connected human network to unite your knowledge brokers in ways they can regularly share ideas and challenge each other on the future of the organization. Without these human-to-human interactions, the flow of ideas and knowledge stops and the organization starts to fall behind those who facilitate this well.

Do You Have Appropriate Mechanisms for Knowledge Co-Creation and Transfer?

The challenge is to know who your knowledge brokers are and proactively connect them so that they can co-create new knowledge. Even if you are not aware of who they are—and they are often not the people around the strategy table dialogue—many high-value creative conversations happen informally. Ideas are created in the nursery of innovation, but ideas then need to be nurtured to germinate into a project that realizes their potential.

In *Where Good Ideas Come From*,[5] Steven Johnson provided many examples of how the potential of creative ideas discussed within informal networks of knowledge brokers was turned into value. In a time when "reading for development" for many is scanning titles and comments on social media, a good title is critical to stimulate potential readers to read beyond the title or review. Johnson's stories highlighted how important connecting different perspectives through creative and exploratory conversations were to the co-creation of new knowledge. Simply sharing existing knowledge will not necessarily create value; it is the adaptation of knowledge to new contexts or applications that brings the opportunities. Traditional teaching is limited to remembering content that is known as a basic form of learning. Such a method does not inherently enable the learner to develop new ways of thinking. This "known" approach is like putting the pieces of a jigsaw puzzle together to recreate the image. However, Johnson was discussing the power of socializing through constructive and challenging conversation. This "sharing" approach is more like taking pieces from many jigsaws and combining them in novel ways that generate an entirely fresh image. This approach enables those in the conversation to co-create new knowledge. New knowledge and insights grow from the interactions between people and is dependent on their level of trust. The higher the level of trust, the more open the conversation, and therefore the greater the potential for novel ideas to emerge. Johnson's story of how GPS was invented is an inspiring example of the effective creation of something completely new through informal interactions. This approach is now being developed into more formal learning environments in which the learning facilitator (I deliberately do not use the term "teacher" to differentiate this approach from traditional approaches of content sharing) engages learners with a concept and stimulates them to explore it. The learning becomes a social experience in which learners bring together their collective experiences and perspectives around the topic and discuss similarities and differences.

I have personally witnessed the benefits of using this approach in both commercial contexts and formal learning environments. It loosely follows the principles of andragogy, a form of adult learning that can be applied in informal or formal learning environments. The principles of andragogy[6] have been known for a long time, but unfortunately have not been commonly or widely applied. These are worth listing briefly as they are key to the success of the knowledge co-creation interactions and the outcomes.

The basic assumptions about adult learners are, as a person matures:

1. Their self-concept moves from being a dependent personality toward being a self-directed human being.

2. Their accumulated experience becomes an increasing resource for learning.

3. Their readiness to learn becomes oriented increasingly to the developmental tasks of their social roles.

4. Their time perspective changes from one of postponed application of knowledge to immediacy of application, and accordingly their orientation toward learning shifts from one of subject-centeredness (theoretical) to one of problem-centeredness (practical application).

5. Their motivation to learn is internal.

Making these assumptions about the people interacting with you generates a totally different mindset. Rather than advocating your position to influence them to do what YOU think is right, you explore with them in a collective sense-making activity to seek to understand. That is, you divergently explore the situation from a wide scope of perspectives and to see it as an opportunity to create a range of options, rather than as a specific problem for which you can find the hidden answer. Our most significant challenges do not yet have solutions as they are not yet fully understood. If you assume THE answer can be discovered for complex situations, you will only be able to approach the challenge in existing known ways. That approach is inadequate in complex situations[7] as each new context requires a unique option, and there may be several of these ranging from poor through to amazingly productive. The best innovations come from applying this emergent approach. Guidelines exist to enable more effective management of this. Design Thinking[8] is one example aligned with this approach as participants collaboratively explore the challenge through a range of lenses and interactive cycles of exploration to create novel options.

Social learning works best when there is a high level of mutual recognition of each other's perspectives and where differences are seen as interesting contrasts to explore rather than as points of conflict. The acceptance of a multiple reality soon emerges, within which apparently contradictory perspectives can be equally right in a human sense-making system. When we accept that my reality is different from your perspective, because we each have different experiences of seeing, we are in a good position to learn from each other. Recent advances in neuroscience[9] have reinforced the observation that our brains are remarkable at filling in unknown gaps.[10] The problem is that we see what we think is there, rather than what is there, and this is influenced by the established pattern that our brain already knows. Two people can look at the same thing and come to an entirely different understanding. This is of course a significant part of why we enjoy magic tricks. The magician is a master of distraction who makes you see what he or she wants you to see, and in doing so the reality of what actually happens is hidden.

The reverse is true in business and organizational development. The magic comes from revealing what others were not able to find or see. Releasing the secret of the innovation drives competitive advantage and sustains performance. When Apple created the smartphone, they did not actually invent any new technology. They created a new concept by combining a range of existing ideas—telephones, mobile music, downloadable files, and touch-sensitive screens, into a cool innovative device. They enabled the magic by providing the spaces and time for their people to explore what might be possible, rather than making a small improvement on what already existed. As Sony and Nokia come to realize, the rest is history. However, it did not take long for a range of new players, led by Samsung, to jump onto the new path and find ways to outsell Apple at their own new game.

As discussed in the previous chapter, knowledge co-creation and flow requires a special environment of trust and a foundation of strong relationships. Leading to enable such an environment requires attention to people and capabilities and providing the freedom to explore and make errors without fear of reprisal. If knowledge brokers feel safe and know they will be supported in a learning environment, they will generate more value than if controlled and micromanaged. Generating the right mix of freedom and responsibility to deliver is a refined art of quality leadership. 3M found out the hard way that too much control reduces experimentation and ultimately damages innovation. Fortunately, a change in leadership reversed the trend by allowing more freedom and restored their innovation leadership. However, too little control can also result in insufficient delivery of commercially viable projects. A clever aspect of Google is their one day per week for employees to work on their own ideas. This is highly motivating as it places trust in the employees' ability to generate new knowledge and leads to many commercial innovations. It generates a wide range of possibilities to be explored, but there is also an expectation that value will be created.

It would be great if there was a simple formula for the right ratio of failures to successes, and an easy indication at what point an idea should be abandoned. However, success and failure are not simple. Experienced entrepreneurs know that failure is inevitable, but they also understand that failures need to happen quickly, cheaply, and early to optimize over-all performance. Most successful entrepreneurs understand that failing is more an investment in the future than a cost. They view failure as a learning process that builds experiences and capabilities that will enhance their performance next time. Ensuring that the ratio of failure to suc-cess remains positive guarantees there is a next time. The most successful entrepreneurs ensure success by engaging a network of knowledge brokers as informal advisors to both challenge and support them. This network is self-determining. Too many high risks and the value losses from failures are likely to outnumber the value generated from successes. However, too few risks and creative experiments, due to overly cautious attitudes, slow the rate of learning and makes the organization uncompetitive.

How Do You Monitor Knowledge Adoption and Effective Application?

The first place anyone seeks advice on progress is from their closest trusted advisors, whether personal friends or professional associates. This happens informally every day in every workplace, through informal social conver-sations. This is natural thing as we are social beings. However, seeking advice from close quarters may not always give the best insights. Those closest to us may not want to provide opinions that may be perceived as negative or critical. Bad news from those we trust can be emotionally challenging because of its social implications. When a romantic partner asks a partner how they look, it is more likely they will get the answer they want to hear, which may or may not be the complete truth. The same can be true for business advice if the relationship is close. Groupthink is a common outcome when constructive criticism is not tolerated or desired. This can result because of perceived risk of negative social consequences, fear of political reprisals, or when political correctness overrides sensible constructive dialogue.

Monitoring the performance of your organization can be challenging for all these reasons. How do you know what to measure, and who do you trust to give you an honest appraisal? Genuine measures of performance are not as objective as it seems and progress is viewed differently by different stakeholder groups. People do business with people! People are fundamentally emotional beings and as such are more influenced by their perceptions than by facts, even though they do not like to acknowledge this. While most business executives argue value is all about the numbers, in reality, performance is more subjective. Listen to the daily stock market report on any news service to hear why the value of businesses changed by billions of dollars. Commentators explain the fluctuations with highly subjective words like sentiment, confidence, and perception of risk, more often than they address the actual operational performance of the business. Of course, both quantitative and qualitative measures are important in the longer term, but the changes in value dramatically shift in the shorter term on the emotional aspects.

Performance can be monitored by listening to the stories told among the people across the organization and by combining these stories with indirect criteria like staff turnover and length of service. Together, they paint a more complete picture. The corridor conversations are reflective of the mood and culture, and provide insights impossible to access without talking regularly to a wide range of people. Although this is hard to assess and very different from how most organizations monitor progress, it is powerful. Actively listening and engaging with the stories to reflect on what they mean provides deep insights. Sense-making is another practice in the art of informed leadership and draws on sentiment behind the stories to deeply understand if the organization is progressing. This reflective approach provides a more truthful understanding of your future-readiness than looking at last month's financial performance.

How do you move mindsets from "What is!" to "What is Possible?"

The most common mindset you encounter in organizations is one that describes "what is happening" or "what just happened." Sharing perspectives of what happened and why is a useful foundation, but this only explains the past. Finding people who can confidently advise how effective something was and what value it has generated is more difficult, and more useful, but still insufficient. Finding people who can provide robust advice on what should happen next and why this is the optimal path is rare, but most needed. A future-focused mentality is somewhat unreliable because it requires extrapolation in the present, based on the past to predict options for the future. It requires the person providing the advice to be confident working in uncertainty and to be prepared to be wrong—or at least inaccurate. Figure 3.1 shows how the degree of certainty rapidly diminishes from the distant past through the present and into the future. The further into the future you need to make a decision for, the less accurate the answers are likely to be. As the pace of change increases, the length and clarity of situational stability decreases. Even within the lifecycle of a medium-term project, what is known (or assumed) at the beginning is often found to be suboptimal and requires adjustment as the project proceeds. This is not necessarily a result of poor planning; it reflects the reality of working in the modern world with its ever-changing foundations. It is also why Agile approaches have become more common, since they can shift to accommodate as new knowledge becomes available. By comparison, traditional stage and gate processes are too rigid to cope with emerging adaptations.

Humans are more comfortable working in a predictable relationship: That is, where there is a defined relationship between cause and effect.

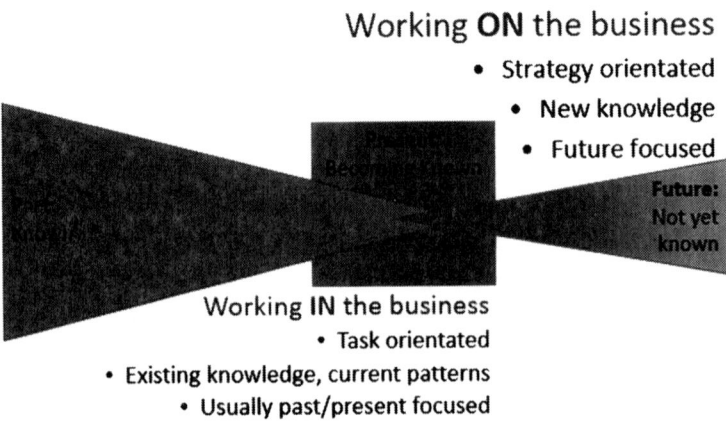

Figure 3.1 *Knowledge and decision making from a certain past to uncertain future*

However, this is not the reality of modern human contexts. One insight from Dave Snowden's Cynefin framework is that while it is possible to retrospectively determine why things happened in complex situations, it is extremely difficult to accurately predict what will happen in future. An example that highlights the unknown aspect of everyday life is the adage "50% of advertising effort is ineffective, we just don't know which 50%." If we knew which half worked, we would not invest in blanket advertising. Monitoring social media traffic and big data analysis is now enabling much better targeting of advertising investment, as opposed to "spend." Logic tells us that the more specific knowledge we have, the more likely we are to assess what is likely to happen. But modern experience demonstrates that your past knowledge can also be the cause of your downfall, because sticking to the same path may no longer be the best way forward.

So...

If accurately predicting the future is inherently difficult, how can we plan for it?

How do we make decisions for the future and then monitor whether they delivered what we expected?

What do we do when we see differences?

These questions highlight the challenges and, at the same time, the opportunities. If this is hard to do and uncertain, then others also have the same difficulties in knowing what will happen. A great deal of money has been made writing simulations to expose leaders and managers to uncertainty so they are better prepared. These learning experiences help to prepare them to deal with unpredictability and to be able to see alternative perspectives and break existing thinking patterns. Deciding what to keep and what to change requires higher-order judgment about trends, probability, risks, and perceptions of social expectations—another art of leadership. This is best achieved by engaging your current knowledge brokers in conversations to constantly and constructively challenge their current knowledge, with an eye on the future and the market trends. Sometimes the genius stroke is to accelerate an existing idea and at other times it is to abandon an existing one and invest in a disruptive innovation.

The key points are to know who your knowledge brokers are and to ensure you are creating the environment where they can discuss differences in a way that avoids conflict. Getting this right leads to the co-creation of new knowledge and pragmatic approaches on how to apply these insights to generate innovation and value. As stated in earlier chapters, this requires a special relationship between the people involved, which must be proactively fostered. When this is achieved, the people involved feel part of something bigger and have a sense of loyalty to the teams they interact with and the organization that made it possible. Such people are more likely to want to stay at the organization. The benefits of these relationships are extended as new knowledge flows into the next cycle of projects and this knowledge is retained and applied. Carrying these relationships and knowledge into the next cycle helps to ensure the series of projects act as stepping stones to an increased foundation of capabilities and learning at individual, team, and organizational levels. In effect, well-led projects that involve the knowledge brokers through-out the strategic cycle not only become vehicles of knowledge transfer, but they also become a collaborative road trip of dedicated people on an inclusive journey to create a more effective future.

Ultimately, the best way to predict your future is to create it with the very best people you can inspire to collaborate with you, before someone else creates your future for you.

Contributor Case Study

Dr. Ricky Tsui, R&D Director, Arup University, East Asia

Continuous Learning Through Projects

The Arup University was established in 2009 and covers:

1. foresight, innovation, and research,
2. knowledge sharing,
3. learning & development, and
4. information management.

The key objective is to holistically manage knowledge creation, sharing to disseminate such that the needs of our daily operations and business practices can be better addressed. The ultimate aim is to maintain the company's competitive edge and build our reputation as a market leader in knowledge, creativity, and innovative design.

Typical projects at Arup require professional colleagues to plan and design buildings or infrastructures that last for many years. In this aspect, foresight studies and works (what I call "Knowledge of the Future") are critical in identifying key drivers and predicting possible scenarios of our future business and working environment. Consistently delivering creative solutions and innovative designs, satisfies current needs and drives future standards and relationships. Our foresight initiatives set us apart and promote Arup as a distinctive thought leader. Clients that come to Arup are seeking innovative and holistic solutions.

Arup conducts hundreds of research projects each year, mostly in collaboration with universities and strategic partners. A strategic research roadmap guides our development direction in categories of "Now, New, and Next."

Knowledge sharing is the key to deliver global skills locally and to provide total solutions to clients. Our staff receives a knowledge handbook, in their preferred language, in their first week with the firm, showing how different basic knowledge brands (Insights, Skills Networks, Arup Projects, Arup People and Essentials), can help them deliver daily work more effectively. Our over 50 skills networks (communities of practice) are actively involved in the entire KM chain from knowledge creation, harvesting, and sharing to embed our collective knowledge into our projects. Various formal and informal sharing and learning activities are driven by skills networks, which monitor industry trends to help set our skills development and research direction. Knowledge harvesting has been done on a regular basis, for example, in "technical burst" section, in which colleagues are invited to present the latest knowledge harvested in client or research projects for a few minutes to board members as well as in the "tech bite" evening sharing events to interested colleagues. Latest Enterprise 2.0 tools have been deployed to enhance working efficiency and help drive creativity and innovation. For example, our in-house developed tools, such as Mail Manager and Qeep, have provided good platforms for managing project correspondence. Yammer and Skills Network Forums facilitate discussion within project teams as well as seeking advice related to specific skills from colleagues around the world.

On learning, Arup University offers three levels of training:

1. Doctoral module: Arup collaborates with local universities to help colleagues work on individual research topics in line with the firms' future development direction.
2. Masters' module: 1-year cross-disciplinary courses on new subjects that are of significant importance to business, in collaboration with renowned universities.
3. Professional module: Technical trainings from 1 hour to a few weeks, run by internal colleagues identified by individual skills knowledge harvested from projects allowing effective knowledge transfer to take place.

The success of Arup is enhanced through a good sharing culture and integrating knowledge, both through our daily operations and business processes and through projects that change us and the clients and communities we serve.

Reflective Activities and Additional Learning Resources for the Curious Executive and Students

Applying this learning in practice

1. Gather a small group of experienced peers and ask which of your recent projects developed knowledge and capabilities that you need for the future. Was this proactively managed or did the benefits just happen? Explore what you can implement in your projects to co-create knowledge within the project to enhance future performance.
2. Use Figure 3.1 to categorize decisions you are currently making that will change the future outlook of the organization. Consider the ratio of decisions that are stimulating enhanced strategic future options compared to those that are for short-term tactics.

3. Review how you analyze both project successes and failures with a view to making genuine improvements in our processes and systems. Challenge the impact these actions are taking and whether the documents you record around such activities are effective or not.

Additional learning resources:

www.intelligentanswers.com.au/KnowledgeSuccession

CHAPTER 4

Why, Who, What, Followed by When, Where, and How

Executive Summary

Chapter 4 explores why the sequence of questions to be asked about projects and organizational performance is critical. It challenges readers to consider long-term tangible outcomes as a bigger part of the equation in planning, rather than considering the project as an independent island. Key points of this chapter are:

- The relationship between outputs and outcomes for ultimate value creation
- The underestimated skills of active listening and constructive challenge
- The relationships and gaps between strategic plans and implementation in practice

Insights to guide optimal questions at the right times in organizational operation and projects include:

1. Sequence of questions is important
2. Questioning and listening
3. Understanding purpose
4. Connecting Vision, Strategy, Doing, and Achieving

Sequence of Questions Is Important

You often hear people say they need to know all about an idea before they can decide to engage with it (or not). This has become more common since Western society has become increasingly litigious and therefore more risk averse. Social and political correctness were needed to make society fairer that it was, but I believe in some cases this has gone too far. Many initiatives are stifled because people are reluctant to discuss the challenges they face in a pragmatic and professional manner. When the ability to take an alternative point of view is suppressed, progress on innovation slows. This is not to say that we should completely disregard cultural and historical aspects of who we are and how things get done. Clearly, they are important and need to be discussed in an open way such that a mutually beneficial path can be found to integrate new ideas into a new future. All cultures evolve overtime, some faster than others. Enabling conversations to explore differences highlights gaps to be acknowledged and managed, or even closed to integrate as a diverse society. However, too often conversations about differences leads to conflict and this should be avoidable when all parties seeks to find common outcomes.

One approach to exploring challenges and opportunities is "The Five W's and How." These are commonly expressed as "Who, What, Where, When, Why, and How" and can assist to determine if an idea is viable and what is the best approach to achieve this. Although this is useful in this format, greater benefit can be achieved by adjusting the order to refine the priority of questions asked.

Starting with What, Where, When, and How focuses attention on the tactical aspects of the initiative, before the strategic value of the potential actions is considered. This is a common practice that results in action-oriented business that does not know where it is going. As discussed in Chapter 2, understanding what the highest priorities are needs to be completed before we can think about what actions to take. A better approach, as seen in Figure 4.1, begins with why, then engages the appropriate people to include their knowledge and expertise (Who) to determine what is the best path. If you have your best and most informed people discussing why something is more critical that others you are in the best position to decide what should be done. This order of questions paves the way toward sustained success by progressing to the next level as better-quality knowledge is shared through a series of stepping stones toward higher-quality decisions. WHY provides the value and priority. WHO provides the knowledge and expertise to get "the right WHAT" and get the "what" right. Once we have value and people sorted, we can then look at processes (How and When) and supporting tools (How,

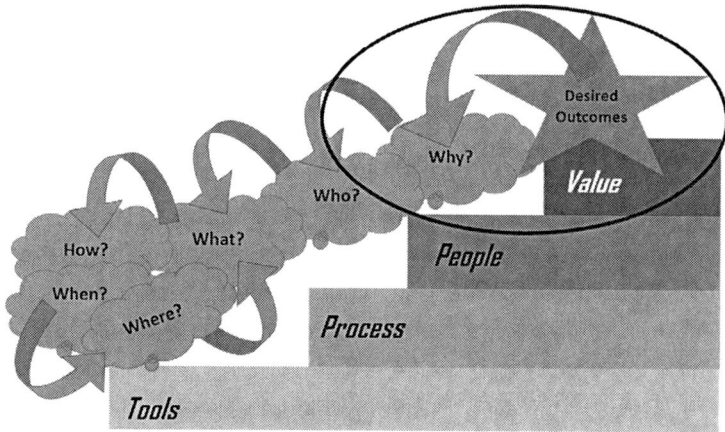

Figure 4.1 Optimal order of conversation to determine priority of potential initiatives

When, and Where). Too often, people muddle the order of the conversation and start with a tool or process and end up doing many things that do not add value, or worse, deflect critical resources away from activities that would have added greater value. Simply asking WHY in a constructive way (with appropriately aligned behavior) can bring priority back into informed decision making and enhance individual, team, and organizational performance. These conversations set the priorities and ensure that precious resources are allocated to the most valuable project that are most aligned with the future direction of the organization. With these insights, the where, when, and how become simpler to resolve.

In the book *Start with WHY*,[1] Simon Sinek appropriately highlighted the sequence stating why, what, how. Perhaps the inclusion of who is implied on the assumption that the right people will be involved in these conversations that connect why to what. However, I believe who is involved is equally as important as why, because only people can judge why. In good organizations this is probably the case and the inspirational leaders Sinek speaks of, are likely to be inclusive and open. However, in my thirty years of professional experience, I observed many organizations where key knowledge brokers are not consulted for the strategic dialogues that set direction and approach. This causes all sorts of inefficiencies and misallocation of resources. Projects that should get implemented are either underfunded or not done at all. Conversely, pet projects of senior stakeholders, which deliver comparatively less value, are often supported. This is why these organizations remain in the average pack rather than among the leaders.

Including key people early in dialogue helps set and understand the wider value and implications of the desired outcomes. In a well-considered "Conversation that Matters,"[2] reflecting on WHY first defines the intangible and tangible reasons for actions and priorities. Engaging knowledge brokers in reflective conversations on WHY explores and challenges the value that comes from the decision and actions. It considers the relative priority of how we invest our time to deliver the most important outcomes and their connection to the longer term. It opens up the assessment of value to include both tangible and intangible aspects that remain after the project is completed and how this builds a foundation for the future. Without pausing to discuss relative priorities, we can quickly sink into the mire of "just doing," because we become focused on being seen to be doing, rather than doing the right things. This is an unfortunate approach to "perception management" in modern organizations, as opposed to building genuine reputation building. That is, acting in strategic and sustainable ways using evidence-based decision making.

An effective leader engages their team with a series of exploratory questions to understand why. They challenge relative benefits of a range of options and leverage the diversity of views available to them to make better informed decisions before acting. This can be done quite quickly—even in minutes in some cases. Done well, it does not cause procrastination or lead to group-think. Not done leads to misalignment and poor performance. The key is to reflect first and in a way that engages rather than threatens those involved. Once you know WHY, your initiative is worthy of priority; by including WHO should be involved in the conversations you can then better determine WHAT should be done. With a clear vision around Why, Who, and What, the when, where, and how becomes obvious.

The ability to ask the right question is more than half the battle of finding the answer. Thomas J. Watson (Chairman and CEO IBM, 1952 to 1984).

Questioning and Listening

There is no sense in asking a question if you are not interested in listening to the answer that others provide. Questions can be extremely powerful and influential, in both positive and negative ways. The way it is asked, the tone, and body language it comes packaged with and the political way in which it is delivered all impact what happens next. Questions come with intent. For best outcomes, this intent can be to genuinely explore the divergence of opinion and the possibilities that others can contribute. The desired outcomes of open and exploratory questions are to inquire to create a range of ideas to solicit better ways to act. Listening is done by all involved. This approach engages participants behind a collective set of actions, builds loyalty, and generates ownership of the next steps. Alternatively, the intent of an aggressively and robustly framed question can be to silence the diversity of views to establish a powerbase and reinforce the hierarchy. These largely rhetorical "questions" are meant to converge the conversation toward the desire of the power player. Their desired outcome is to have others listen to their advocated point of view and then act the way the controlling leader wants. Unless there is a crisis of extenuating circumstances, this approach disengages participants from the prescribed actions and relies on compliance to be implemented, as the participants do not have a sense of identity and ownership of the next steps. Listening is practiced by the participants, but not the advocate.

There is a place for both advocacy and inquiry.[3] As stated in the previous section of this chapter, order is important. Start with inquiry by posing questions to explore options, solicit insights, and co-create new knowledge. Follow with advocacy to influence others, listen to, and support decision taken about the best of the options generated and why they are superior. Edward de Bono suggested "Yellow before Black"[4] is more productive (yellow as creative thinking for inquiry, before black as critical thinking to advocate). This is also consistent with the Appreciative Inquiry[5] approach, which supports securing agreement on longer-term mutual outcomes, before focusing on tasks to be acted on. The consistency in these approaches is the iterative cycles of divergent thinking to generate strategic outcomes followed by convergent thinking to reduce the list of possibilities to one of a few tasks or projects to be implemented. This approach is also included in a range of proprietary models and also in Design Thinking[6] approaches.

The real strength of these approaches is they are human-centric and involve social interactions that creatively explore options in cycles to drive innovation solutions. This by necessity involves iterative cycles of questioning to challenge and listening to constructively challenge and make judgment. Sometimes people consider judgment to be an unfair or overly controlling characteristic, and this can be the case when it is inappropriately used. That is, without being proceeded by an open and honest inquiry. The basis of the entire Western legal system is (theoretically) based on such cycles. However, it too is sometimes deliberately overcomplicated in order to advocate rather than assess a balanced argument. Of course, this impacts the quality of the judgments made.

A great insight about genuine listening can be gained from the traditional Chinese character for listening. The traditional characters were symbolic and representative of the actions they described. The listen character includes wider aspects of truly "hearing" (that is, understanding the sense and meaning of what is being shared). The left side of the symbol represents an ear and the right side represents the individual or "you" and includes images representing eyes, undivided attention, and heart. This symbol highlights that when actively listening we use multiple senses. Ears for sound and words are supplemented with eyes to watch body language and maintain eye contact to maintain undivided attention and to feel and be empathetic. Engaging in genuine active listening inevitably triggers further questions to inquire in an effort to understand more. Effective communication is not just "transmission," it includes cycles of transmission, receipt, interpretation, and reflection in order to generate action and response. Responding before hearing the whole message or without reflecting on what it means is disrespectful and limits the opportunity to build a stronger relationship with the other parties.

Building a culture of critical and respectful listening and questioning is art of quality leadership.

It is driven by being a role model for these by demonstrating them through your own practice.

Understanding Purpose

Purpose can be a very cliché, especially when used in a shallow manner. It can also be an extremely powerful and life-changing question to pose of yourself, your team, or your organization. Carl Jung advocated that only through deep inquiry of one's own integrity could one truly understand our motivations and purpose.[7] Jung believed that we all contain a subconscious battle of "good and evil" which greatly influences our conscious decision making and actions. The exploration of your real motives is a difficult challenge to do objectively, because of the inherent subconscious subjectivity driving who we are and what we do. The same can be stated for organizations. Without a deliberate and constant challenge and confirmation of their purpose, the organization can amble along and stay from the destiny they desire. This is especially so when as organizations, and governments, now undergo more frequent changes in their leadership. The shorter the term of leadership, the greater the incentive for the leaders to make changes that create short-term benefits at the expense of longer term. This is primarily because they are judged and rewarded on the impacts they "achieve" during their tenure, with no regard for the value they create or destroy in the longer term. Worthwhile capability, like trust, takes a long time to build and only moments to destroy. I once witnessed a restructure of an organization where a medium-sized business lost 200 years of internal core knowledge on one day. These represented core skills, knowledge, experiences, and history in a small number of long-term employees of a specific unit. The argument was proposed that this company had never experienced a public recall and this was as a result of the capabilities and experiences these people brought to the table. They effectively were an assurance for success. This argument was rejected and the resources were "released" to realize a short-term profit and a significant bonus for the "leader" of the restructuring project. That project manager went on to secure similar roles in other organizations and the organization left behind suffered three public recalls of product in the next 12 months due to mistakes made by inexperienced personnel and procedures that no longer were done.

Faster churn across generations of leadership is a double-edged sword. It can prevent the organization from becoming stale and disconnected and at the same time can destroy the organizations by reducing its purpose. Most people want to passionately contribute to an organization that they believe in. It drives a sense of meaning for them and provides a community they are proud to belong to. Once this purpose is removed or constantly changing, it is hard for them to maintain the passion. The Progress Principle[8] provided the hard evidence to support what good leaders already subconsciously knew about why people want to actively participate and what they leave. That is, the primary motivating factor at work is doing meaningful work. The biggest demotivating factor is when leaders do not know what meaning work for you is and why. It does not matter whether the work is ongoing routine activities or change projects, people want to be involved in decision making and be considered valued.

People who buy-into your purpose remain loyal dedicated workers who create value. Those who don't understand your purpose, or reject it, are less productive, disengaged, or simply don't remain.

Connecting Vision, Strategy, Doing, Achieving

There is no shortage of books on each of these four topics, ranging from great to ordinary and from old to new. Mostly they contain similar messages: Create a vision to set the direction, enable this vision through an aligned strategy that allocates resources to the priority initiatives, and generate a program of detailed plans of actions (doing) in order to achieve sustained success. Given this is absolutely clear and consistent, why do so many organizations and projects fail to deliver their stated aims?

Sometimes it is a result of bad luck. Sometimes it is because through no fault of their own, the world just changes or perhaps they took too many risks, resulting in a negative ratio of successes to failures. These are all plausible explanations that can happen. However, the most fundamental and common reason for ongoing underperformance is disconnected complacency, demonstrated by simply not connecting the vision to the strategy to form plans and act on them with discipline. The flow of knowledge and action was already discussed in detail in Chapter 2. However, it is worthwhile reinforcing in this series of comments of the critical importance of these connections through entire cycles. One of the biggest issues in most "climate surveys" (assessments of the "health" of the organization via all employee survey) is lack of communication:

- How can managers support the vision and purpose of the organization if the leaders did not effectively communicate what they meant?
- How can project team members decide on priorities for decisions and know who to transfer their knowledge to in a handover to operations if they don't understand the strategy?
- How can efficient plans be made if there was no prioritization of resources for the key projects?
- How can we achieve anything if all these questions are not consistently answered?

Asking the right questions gives us the information, knowledge, and insights we need to achieve is a point made earlier. Questions are how we fix the communication gap (see Chapter 12) and clarify what we don't know, but need to. Questions are how we connect the layers of the organization's operations through the layers of orientation from Vision to strategy to plans to achieving outcomes. Lack of communication is one of the biggest barriers to this flow (and sometimes in overly political organizations, deliberate miscommunication can create havoc). A powerful set of questions is the best utility you have in your kit. For a leader it is a set of open questions to stimulate divergent exploration to generate opportunities. For a manager it is a mixed set of open and closed questions that enable refining down to the root cause of problem to be resolved. As Stephen Covey so eloquently advised, "First seek to understand."

Just having the questions is insufficient to generate high performance, there needs to be appropriate actions taken once the most suitable answers are found. The world is littered with organizations who "know what they should do," but simply do not act on this in time to convert the potential into value.

Regularly ask yourself, am I doing the most valuable thing I could be right now? (and for whom?)

If so, keep doing it! If not drop what you are doing and do the more important thing.

Contributor Case Study

Randhir Pushpa, Unisys, India

Knowledge and Innovation

There is an ongoing debate on the relationship between KM and Innovation. There are many that say that KM helps innovation, while some say that KM hampers Innovation. Here we present a case study where KM concepts were leveraged to build a culture of Innovation. The deliver center (with a delivery unit of around 800 employees) of Unisys focuses on developing software, based on requirements. The kind of work that this deliver center produces has high level of innovation content and hence the delivery team was expected to have a culture of innovation and innovativeness. The KM team was responsible for building a culture of innovation.

To promote a culture of innovation, the KM team focused on promoting patenting by motivating their employees to patent their intellectual assets. For this, a mixture of a culture of knowledge sharing, building thought leadership, collaboration, and rewarding activities was adopted.

Culture of knowledge sharing: Having a knowledge sharing culture, which helps employees connect easily with each other, get the relevant knowledge faster, and solve their problems easily, is important. The focus was on developing a culture of sharing through technical talks, social networking platforms, and cross training. As the culture of sharing spread, employees found it easy to connect with SMEs. Withholding knowledge became low and employees felt comfortable sharing as well as asking for information.

Thought Leadership: For employees to innovate, not only should they be well connected, but they should also continuously refresh and update their knowledge on the latest in their field. To promote this high level of learning, we focus on paper contests. The contests, which were themed around innovation, required employees to write innovative ideas that they had and work with research institutes, enabling employees to work with researchers, instilling a research culture. As a result of these professional connections, a sense of researching, focus, and innovation for learning was created.

Evangelization on patenting: Since the culture of innovation was created through evangelizing of patenting, we had many sessions that explained the process of patenting; how patenting helps an individual and the organization, what can be patented, and the rewards. The inventors were rewarded and communication on the same was shared across the organization.

Support team to promote patenting: An ecosystem of all interested parties was brought together to ensure all collaborated to promote patenting, including Managers, Attorneys, HR, Finance, Payroll, and others. Inventors who had already filed were also asked to share their knowledge on the patenting process. Along with this we leveraged knowledge of prolific inventors, who worked as "Sniffers" and identified innovative ideas. Inventors were also welcomed to reopen their ideas if they saw merit in it.

Motivation through Celebration: To ensure that employees stayed motivated, along with financial rewards, the employees were given certificates called "All hands meet." A "Wall of Fame" was also set up in the office to highlight success stories.

Success: Within a short period of 4 years, the patent productivity of employees increased drastically. Currently, this small team contributes around 25 percent of the patents filed by the organization.

Reflective Activities and Additional Learning Resources for the Curious Executive and Students

Applying this learning in practice

1. Create a list of questions that should have been asked, or asked earlier for your failed projects. Discuss why these questions were not asked and what the impact could have been if they were. Build the list of questions and start asking them in project planning rather than after the errors.

2. Challenge yourself at the beginning of each new initiative to define the value to be created, or losses to be avoided and who will receive that benefit. Cross check this with the potential risks. Although this sounds very logical, the lack of robust questioning and divergent thinking early in projects is a serious problem that benefits from such direct action with a colleague, how much of your time is spent on routine tasks, and how much is invested on change activities. Consider whether this ratio of time is adequate for you to remain competitive with the pace of change in your industry sector.

3. Make a list of the tools and processes that have been implemented in your organization and discuss the purpose of these. Ask whether they are effective and whether they deliver the stated benefits that were used to justify their implementation.

Additional learning resources:

www.intelligentanswers.com.au/KnowledgeSuccession

CHAPTER 5

People Have Knowledge, Relationships Generate Value

Executive Summary

Chapter 5 explores the importance of the human elements of project management and the impacts these have on performance. Key points of this chapter are:

- Stakeholders are to be engaged and involved, not silenced and "managed."
- Communications plans are often written and not delivered and too often only one-way "broadcasts" rather than participative multidirectional dialogue.
- The world is paradoxical, requiring project managers to be highly adaptive and do seemingly opposite things at the same time for different purposes.
- Ultimately, projects are about capability development and this is often lost to people outside the organization.

Engaging people to co-create value benefits from fostering trusted relationships and sharing knowledge. These in turn are accelerated by paying close attention to:

1. Stakeholders;
2. Communicating project outcomes and outputs;
3. Maintaining engagement and participation;
4. Leading AND Managing; and
5. Action learning and collaborative development.

Stakeholders

The word "stakeholders" is expressed at board and project meetings all the time. However, in my experience there is LOT more talk about stakeholders than reflection and actions. In the worst cases, they get confused with sponsors, shareholders, team members, and "them"—that generic collective term used to describe others who must be appeased, but are considered disruptive to your work. The simplest definition, and there are many, in organizational and project contexts is *any individual or party who is impacted (positively or negatively) by your activities or can impact your plans.* This is necessarily inclusive of a wide range of individuals and groups, especially when implementing change projects (are there any effective projects that are not change projects?). It includes all of the terms used earlier and also groups often missed in significant change programs, such as customers and consumers (internal and external), communities, and family members.

Stakeholders are critical for success of all work,[1] be it business as usual or project related. When stakeholders are actively involved in your project, even as part of the planning processes before the project actually starts, they can generate their biggest benefits. Proactively engaging your stakeholders in your project generates ownership for the outcomes. Engaging stakeholders initially is much easier to manage than getting them to buy in after the project is completed when they knew nothing of it, or worse, were actively kept out of the decision-making processes that determined its direction and outputs.

Engaging stakeholders is discussed in greater depth in Chapter 12, so it is only mentioned briefly here. As with all topics in this book, everything is intimately connected to everything else, a framework is needed that helps to scaffold the structure and connect the concepts. However, in creating this simplified structure or "roadmap" of how things connect with each other, we also overly simplify the reality of the situation. This book could easily be structured in many ways, and as different people read it, they may well explore it from a variety of directions. The same is true for stakeholders. They can be assessed and categorized in many ways by your team, so that you know who is who and how they are best engaged. Unless you actually engage with stakeholders to understand who they are and why they are important, this is just a series of untested perceptions. This provides the opportunity to determine their stance toward your project and their level of influence on your work. If you plot stakeholders on a scale of influence in the organization on one axis and support for your project on the other, you can categorize them into Sponsors and Allies (high influence and support), Enthusiasts (low influence, high support), Opponents or Adversaries (high influence, low support or aggressively against), and Watchers (low influence and support). See the exercise at the end of this chapter for a fun way to explore this. This provides a relatively simple way to approach a complex and fluid factor, so you must take care to continuously reassess the stakeholders and ensure their relationships with you and your work remain solid.

> *Everything should be made as simple as possible, but not simpler.*
> —Albert Einstein

Simplifying is necessary to help in understanding, but too many modern managers try to oversimplify and, in doing so, lose track of what is important. Tasks can be simplified reasonably well and processes refined in great detail to make them more efficient. However, the same is not true of stakeholders. Making assumptions about the needs and desires of stakeholders is one of the most error-prone aspects of leading and managing. Human beings are social creatures who need to be engaged rather than managed. This requires inclusion not exclusion and listening to, and informing rather than being told. Not doing this is a significant cause of failure in both business-as-usual processes and in projects.

Communicating Project Outcomes and Outputs

In climate surveys (organizational cultural assessments), poor leadership and inadequate communication are usually among the most common challenges. People often have the perception that they are not being fully informed, especially in times of significant change. They usually cynically blame "the leadership" for this lack of communication. Timing and mode of communication are critical to perceptions of inclusiveness for the stakeholders, and all organizations have mistimed or poorly worded a communication, or sent it out to the wrong target audience at some stage. Such incidents can be difficult to recover from, so are best avoided by investing in planning. Of course, you don't know what to communicate with whom until you know who your stakeholders are. Once you have your stakeholder list and have assessed their impacts on your project or initiatives, you then need to assess how to best communicate. This is not your comprehensive list of target audience members: It is a list of discrete target audiences, as different members in the list will need to be engaged in ways appropriate to them. Senior leaders may want regular personal face-to-face, two-way dialogue and other more distant stakeholder groups may be content just being informed as key milestones are met. The frequency and level of detail in your communications will vary by stakeholder or stakeholder group in different phases of the project or process. Your more strategic stakeholders (such as sponsors and senior decision makers) will want to know about longer-term outcomes (intangible impacts beyond the project itself, such as cultural development). More tactical stakeholders (such as a machine operator or data entry administrator) will be more interested in the outputs (more immediate tangible and measurable deliverables, such as exactly when do they stop using the existing method and start using the new tool or process).

Note I stated communicate *with* stakeholders, rather than *to* stakeholders. Simple words matter as language carries great meaning, as discussed in Chapters 8 and 9. "Communication" is a generic word that means many things to different people, and this can lead to great misunderstandings. Some mistakenly think that sending an e-mail is "communication." It is, in fact, just one option in the communication process. An e-mail—or voicemail, report, or other similar information or content-based object—can be broadcast to an audience. Broadcast is just the outward bound part of a proper communication process. Broadcasting is like television or radio. The sender does not truly know if the intended audience actually receives the signal. There may be many reasons why this broadcast information was never received, let alone understood and acted upon. The act of dispatching some content to a target audience does not constitute effective communication, even if you did get your list right. The better aligned the mode of delivery is with your target audience's preferences, language, and frequency of receipt, the more likely the message will be received, understood, and hopefully acted upon as desired. However, this is also not sufficient to constitute a full communication cycle. If only partially completed, it is more likely to disengage stakeholders than engage them, or worse, cause blame and conflict.

Effective communication is a full cycle that includes broadcast, receipt, confirmed understanding from the target audience, and then a reply to affirm appropriate actions were taken. The reply may include some evidence and performance indication of how well this has been done. For example, if I wanted a critical action to be performed by a colleague, I would first talk with them to advise what I wanted done and what this would involve. Depending on the experience level of the target and the nature of the activity, this conversation may involve an example output with performance standards defined and a description of desired outcomes. I then follow this up with a written message (such as e-mail, request in a task management system, and action point in meeting minutes) requesting a reply to confirm completion. Such a complete cycle with all details is not usually done in daily operations. When such processes are in place in critical projects, they are often seen as overly bureaucratic. People see such detail as excessive micromanagement and unnecessary for most people as this detail is targeted at the lowest common denominator, and yet if such details are not observed, people argue that the communication is not clear or sufficient.

In reality, stakeholders perceive the quality of communication from their own perspective and this is usually based on subjective assessments rather than objective analysis. This is why stakeholder engagement and effective communications are challenging and worth investing in to get right from the beginning. If you create relationships where clarifying questions are asked in constructive ways, performance increases. If your communications result in a perception of closed, guarded, and "needs to know" basis, your stakeholders are likely to feel disengaged. In such situations, they can start to work against the objectives of your project, as they do not identify themselves as part of the team. Identity, belonging, and buy-in are all covered in more detail elsewhere in the book.

Maintaining Engagement and Participation

Having invested in creating a comprehensive and well-structured stake-holder list and crafted effective communications, you are well on the path of maintaining engaged and participative stakeholders. While you should not try to manage the stakeholders themselves, you must manage your communications so that you manage their expectations. It is far easier to create a path and guide your stakeholders on this shared path than to constantly adjust directions because of poorly planned initiatives. The more you shift the plan, the more difficult it becomes to maintain the trust and loyalty of those involved. However, as stated in earlier chapters, the future is being created as we act and is unpredictable, so change is inevitable. Making early agreements on flexible approaches, such as Agile, ensures expectations remain in line with your initiatives. Stakeholders' expectations are highly volatile in complex environments. As changes start to challenge stakeholders' understanding of outcomes, relationships can become somewhat strained. This is where the interdependencies between leadership, communication, experiences, and expectations can be your biggest asset or your worst nightmare.

The short answer is the greater the changes to plans and the shorter the intervals in which these changes happen, the more the leadership needs to communicate plan adjustments (or lack thereof) to the stakeholders. A common error is waiting to know more detail and with more certainty before communicating. Delaying communications makes people frustrated; they believe those who know what is going on are not informing them. It is usually better to share the fact that you do not know, as most people, but not all, are contented when you share what you do know. This manages expectations and keeps them feeling included. Saying nothing will most often create a divide, as no information often is misread as not being fully informed. Such situations quickly reduce trust and start triggering independent actions that may be counterproductive, or in poorly managed emergency situations, cause panic.

Keeping the stakeholder actively participating in conversations about new information and possible adjustments because of insights and knowledge generated as the initiative progresses is extremely powerful. It can lead to enhanced outcomes and keep the stakeholders' expectations aligned with what is happening in the project. Without proactive maintenance and engagement, the gap between leadership and the stakeholder widens. If left too long, this leads to conflicts and poor performance.

Contributor Case

NASA Optical Design Lab (ODL) at Goddard Space Flight Center

Dr. Joseph Howard, Optical Engineer Optics Branch, NASA/Goddard Space Flight Center
Dr. Juan Roman, Instrument Systems & Technology Division, NASA/Goddard Space Flight Center

Optical design is a critical part of NASA's Goddard Space Flight Center's development of world-class telescopes and science instrumentation for remote spaced-based sensors. With each new instrument concept, scientists will typically first consult an optical designer to both interpret the science requirements and layout potential design forms. Previously at Goddard, recruiting a designer would require getting approval through the engineering chain of command, but that process was streamlined through the establishment of a customer-oriented process dubbed the "Optical Design Lab," or ODL. Now a new customer gets a team of designers, ensuring multiple viewpoints and a better concept upon completion of the task.

The ODL provides an entry point for scientists at Goddard to develop their instrument concepts using a concurrent engineering team-based approach, where multiple disciplines (including the customer scientists and mechanical engineers) are brought into the design process early on where they have influence on the final design in real time during the trade studies. Examples of this include bringing in alignment and test specialist to help influence the system layout to ensure access to metrology points to verify a proper system build, or an opto-mechanical engineer to give feedback on the best form of mechanism for budgeted mass and performance requirements.

A by-product of this team approach to design is the increased exposure of multiple projects on the designers. This raises the overall experience level of the pool of designers that staff the ODL, and it increases awareness across the organization of the multiple missions being considered for future space flight. The greatest long-term payoff is perhaps the anchoring of the institutional knowledge across the center for the best practices in optical design.

One of the first tools developed in the ODL was the establishment of an "optical design database," which is a central repository of optical designs for instruments that go back several decades. Retrieving the data required reaching out to the many individuals who worked those projects, who over the years became the historical caretakers of the documentation. This dispersed knowledge was then converted to a common format, and made both searchable and accessible to all users of the ODL. This database now provides a ready reference to quickly answer questions such as "didn't we make something like that before?" In one recent example, a customer's requirements for a spectrometer observing asteroids were found to be very similar to a previously built planetary flyby imager found in the database. As such, significant time was saved during this study by using the database design as a starting point. This timesaving prevented "re-inventing the wheel," which then allowed more time to address significant issues such as package size and mass for the instrument. Ultimately, a better design was produced for the customer for the time committed to the instrument study.

Leading and Managing

It has often been stated that we should lead people and manage tasks. There is a lot of wisdom in this insight, although it can be a challenge to achieve. What is clear is we do need to BOTH lead and manage at the right time in the right context in order to be successful. We need to lead to determine optimal direction to achieve long-term strategic outcomes. It involves creative divergent thinking to explore options and assess the potential paths and decide on who to involve in the priority initiatives. It also benefits from challenging to ensure the organization has not over-committed across too many initiatives—an often forgotten aspect of quality leadership. Once these things are decided, we then need to switch our leadership thinking cap to the hardhat of management. Management ensures actions and resources are optimally leveraged in a coordinated manner to achieve priorities efficiently and effectively and produce the desired outputs within the agreed timeframes. If you lead without managing, you end up in a dream world of desired outcomes that never eventuate. If you manage without leading, you may do many things, but they may not be the optimal things that need to be done.

Figure 5.1 shows key differences between leading and managing. Management is very structured and focused with a predominant mindset of convergent focus. Metaphorically, the body language of a manager doing excellent management is leaning in to analyze the detail of a problem or opportunity to make a decision that generates action and output. This cycle is repeated and measured to ensure the right number of actions that lead to delivery within the appropriate time, quality, scope, and cost. Resource utilization is carefully monitored and tasks scrutinized to ensure they are both efficiently and effectively executed. Figure 5.1 shows management to be clear, structured, precise, concise, and focused as well as involving the many skills that managers use to simplify situations in assessing, analyzing, and applying decisions to create value. This is the engine room of individual, team, and organizational performance.

By contrast, Figure 5.1 shows the leadership side to be complex, unstructured, colorful, and often somewhat confusing. Leading is a divergent cerebral and emotional exploration seeking to ask questions to find

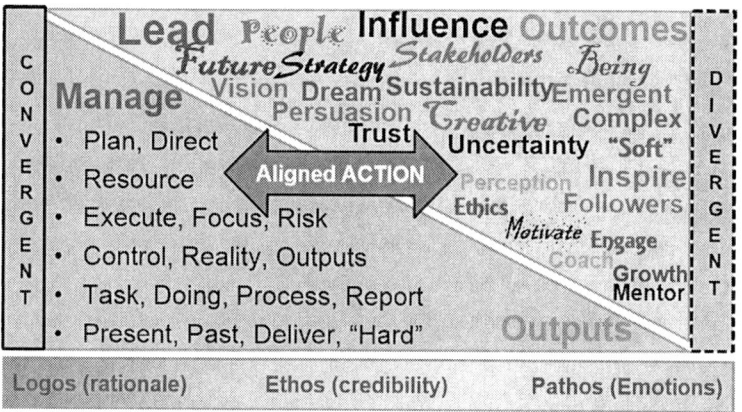

Figure 5.1 The Paradox of leading AND managing

possible options. Unlike management, which is about following the clear path that we know is best, leadership is about finding new paths that take us in new directions, to secure new outcomes. This ambiguity and uncertainty uncovers and mines richness from the unknown future. Leadership actually defines the future through the decisions taken. The quality of leadership is assessed in hindsight by the performance it brings. This is the soft side of who we are as humans. Where management focuses on task and rationale to produce tangible outputs, leadership explores possibilities, people, and relationships to create options with beneficial outcomes. Figure 5.1 highlights this is the "messy" part of performance that is complex and hard to navigate. Compared with management, leadership has little structure and involves taking risks rather than controlling them and their consequences. This is where the creativity and learning happen to generate completely new ideas and fuel innovation.

This does not imply that leaders never need to manage or that managers never need to lead. All successful people need to be able to switch between both when it is clear that the other is required to progress. In a crisis, people are better served by acting than by creatively exploring a wide range of options. Equally when a project is not going well, a wise manager knows to take a step back and consider what other options may be more appropriate. While writing this book, I was swapping between the two very regularly to balance the rational with emotions such as passion and creativity to share the optimal blend of ideas in practical ways. On days when I was investing too much time exploring possibilities, I needed to consciously challenge myself by asking how many new ideas could I fit in each section, concluding I should just put my head down and write before my mind moved on to yet another idea and the old one was lost. Having written a piece, I would then go back over the ideas and assess whether they flowed well and had sufficient diversity to be useful, but not prescriptive. It is important to be consciously aware of which mindset you are deploying and whether it is aligned with the immediate situation and with the longer-term outcomes.

This thinking is not new; Aristotle wrote in "Rhetoric"[2] (4th century BCE) that all three aspects, Ethos, Pathos and Logos, must be in balance to persuade others (see Chapter 12). What is leadership if it does not persuade others to follow? If management is the engine room, leadership is the navigation deck. We need leadership AND management to be effective, and we benefit from being able to nimbly switch between them.

Action Learning and Collaborative Development

We all know that the best learning happens as a result of experience. Yet, most organizations persist in spending more money on classroom-based training rather than investing in well-structured workplace learning approaches. History and research both demonstrate that learning experiences involving application of the learning in the workplace, during or soon after the activities, result in enhanced retention and better outcomes. This applies across the range of learning activities, whether it were creating a better stakeholder management process, crafting better communications to engage more effectively, or becoming a better leader or a more effective manager. Some organizations are beginning to adopt the 70:20:10 (experiential: social: formal) approach[3] to building capabilities: This is working well where it becomes a well-supported initiative with reflective cycles to confirm the effectiveness of the development. Action learning and collaborative development involve learners engaging in experiences where they co-create new knowledge through social interactions and constructive challenges. When real contexts in workplaces are well facilitated with a deliberate emphasis on the learning and knowledge creation to be generated though the process, the value equation changes for all involved, compared to just doing project for the outputs of the project itself. Leveraging projects as active learning and collaborative development opportunities enables you to build strategic foundations to take new opportunities that you did not have when you embarked on the project. Projects can be a steep learning curve for your people and the organization if they are planned that way. If they are not consciously planned as such, some informal learning still occurs, but what happens remains hidden, as the learning gained by the people in the project is not visible. Too often the learning is paid for by your organization, but is lost when members of the team move on to their next contract. It is not only the capabilities that are valuable. Many intangible aspects enhance future performance if managed well. Social connections, knowledge of the organization structures, and strategic relationships with stakeholders and leaders can all dissolve after an initiative without deliberate efforts to maintain them.

Adopting an interactive learning approach in all workplace activities helps to build a stronger sense of meaning and understanding across the organization. It shifts the emphasis from *what* (content, the theories, and the contexts) to asking *why* and *how* is value created or destroyed from the perspective of deeper insights and wider perspectives. These broader and deeper experiences shared through learning communities enable richer dialogue and interactions that enhance performance. Actively engaging learners in peer-to-peer learning similar to that described by Knowles, Holton, and Swanson[4] has taken the learning experience to a higher level and results in greater understanding of the importance of relationships. When you ask project team members what they remember from good and poor project experiences, they usually reflect on the relationships in the team and between teams and stakeholders more than any tangible aspect of the project approach or procedures. These are the aspects that motivate individuals to participate more actively and generate better individual learning outcomes.

One advantage of interactive learning environments is that team members can capitalize on the diversity of cultural backgrounds and disciplines to cross-fertilize ideas. Such proactive environments reinforce learning and enrich insights through a social discovery process of sharing perspectives to create a better future. The quality of interactions can be enhanced through activities such as exploratory games and role-plays to explore the best and worst outcomes of complex scenarios. This reinforces the benefits of generating options for future realistic scenarios, rather than only considering theoretical solutions. If participants reflect on what occurred after each activity, they can maximize their learning and their approach for future situations. Critically reflecting on peers' perspectives develops our capabilities to challenge uncertain concepts and contexts. Participants in such learning activities develop confidence to engage in collaborative dialogue and think for themselves about decisions and actions in their workplaces. This reflective style of development contributes to professional capability and personal strengths, aligning with McIntosh's recommendations for reflective practitioners.[5]

Contributor Case Study

Dr. Alex Bennet, Mountain Quest Institute, USA

Alive with the Fire of Shared Understanding

At the turn of the century, the U.S. Department of the Navy was leading implementation of Knowledge Management (KM), well on its way to becoming the first public sector organization to be recognized as a Most Admired Knowledge Enterprise for "leadership of its knowledge based programs and initiatives, and for its emphasis on organizational learning."

The Department is a complex system with 700,000 plus direct employees, over a million support contractors worldwide, and, unlike other military services, encompassing surface, submarine, air, and land forces. While line authority is a powerful tool in the military, most often the best knowledge resides at the point of action where the commander's intent must be translated and acted upon in rapidly changing, often uncertain and increasingly complex situations. The good news is that there is high social capital. Military members flow in and out of various positions in two- or three-year cycles, and carry a high level of trust for their colleagues. The challenges lay in geographic dispersion, operational diversity, technological inconsistencies, and receptivity to change. ***How to inculcate this learning and catapult to the next level?***

KM implementation was led at the highest levels of the organization. In the role of Chief Knowledge Officer (CKO) was the Deputy Chief Information Officer for Enterprise Integration, Alex Bennet. The linking of KM and Organizational Learning (OL) with Information Management (IM) and Information Technology (IT) provided close connections with the well-supported information management and technology thrusts enabling KM and OL. Working below the Secretariat, Alex was at the helm of a community of practice of over 150 people—in uniform and civilian—representing every major command and situated at different levels of the enterprise.

The initial idea emerged from the CKO team: Create a point in time where every command had access to every KM initiative underway in the Department, what she described as an ***Event Intermediation,*** formally defined as a strategic event used to bring about large-scale change across the enterprise and its larger stakeholder group. This intermediation would connect knowledge seekers with knowledge sources by relating, researching, validating, reshaping, and transferring information, facilitating both vertical and horizontal sharing of knowledge at a point in time as part of larger change strategy.

It was recognized that such an event needed to engage the whole self-body, mind, emotions, and soul, that inner thread of altruism that runs through a Defense organization. ***A Knowledge Fair.*** What this concept meant emerged from the rich diversity of the community and their various support teams, with ideas streaming into reality and the event rapidly took shape. *Commitment:* Hosted by the Secretary of the Navy. Invite senior leaders from every command and capture them on short videos talking about what their commands are doing in KM. Set up DoN team booths to facilitate direct sharing of stories, processes, and technologies that are working and under development (with visitors leaving with the processes, support software, and contacts for continued interaction). *Access:* Hold the Fair in a major Washington, D.C. conference facility and invite representatives of other government organizations delving into KM; if they have products to offer, include booths. A government ID is the entry ticket. The DoN is part of a larger whole; share all we are learning. *Appreciative Inquiry:* Identify teams within the organization where successful actions are happening and highlight these. Have senior leaders visibly reward these accomplishments. *Attention:* Using guided robots as greeters; have veterans in uniform share their learning stories and experiences (complete with pictures); demonstrate new technologies with visitor participation; have palm readers introduce the palm pilot concept; introduce Smart Card technology. *Learning:* Presentations by world experts on the half hour throughout the day; have a magician teach a trick, demonstrate the difficulty of sharing tacit knowledge; hold a pilot Reverse Auction (new eBusiness pricing tool) with Abe Lincoln one of the bidders; engage visitors in creating learning games. *Sustainability:* Develop a virtual CD for distribution across the Department and the larger US government; distribute widely and provide open access via Internet to include: Sharing leadership commitment; Interviewing booth teams and providing synopses and contact information; capturing short discussions from leaders of featured initiatives; highlighting award winners (what, how, and contact info); distributing key thoughts of expert presenters with support materials; transferring developed training and learning materials; distributing DoN toolkits.

The Secretary of the Navy, arrived early, reviewed the booths, individually greeted and thanked each participant, presenting each with a certificate of appreciation, and challenged the Department to restructure and change so as to fully benefit from all the KM development going on today. "As we walk around the Fair we see excellent, excellent systems and processes, but most of it is fairly recent and has not yet been propagated throughout the Department. That is a real challenge." The Fair made a leap forward in meeting that challenge. As the Secretary cut the ribbon officially opening the Fair, he challenged the Department to move into the future as he shared a quote from inventor Charles Kettering. "I am always very interested about the future because I am going to spend the rest of my life there."

Event Intermediation—tapping into the intellectual capital of sailors, Marines, and civilians to link sources with users—became part of the larger continuous change strategy. For example, in 2002, the CKO and CIO team "imagineered" a new type of facility where teamwork and collaboration could be learned and practiced and subjected to scientific inquiry. The core value of sharing was integral to the success DoN was enjoying in pioneering concepts of KM. They produced a formal book that shared the experiences and insights as they constructed and implemented their agenda in KM, Organizational Learning, Information Management, and Information Technology. Much like the Fair, the book started with people throughout the Department, became part of the larger change strategy, and by the time it was printed by the Government Printing Office and distributed throughout the U.S. government, there were over 600 individual contributors and numerous working groups, teams, communities of practice, and communities of interest who contributed to making the DoN KM, OL, IM, and IT strategy a success.

In 2005, the international KM magazine *Inside Knowledge* decided to see what happened in the DoN when their CKO left, resulting in publication of a case study of the DoN, "The Art of War: Empowering frontline decision making." At that point in time, the editor, Simon Lelic, summarized what continues today, "This month's cover story details what can confidently be described as the **most comprehensive and far-reaching knowledge-management initiative every attempted anywhere in the world** ... KM has ... become a fundamental aspect of the way the US Department of the Navy operates ... From the highest to the lowest ranks, from the corridors of Washington, DC to the frontline of military engagement, **there is a prevailing understanding that knowledge, and by extension knowledge management, is everyone's business.**"

Reflective Activities and Additional Learning Resources for the Curious Executive and Students

Applying this learning in practice

1. Create a list of all stakeholders and categorize them against the criteria of support for your activities and level of influence using a scale from minus three to plus three, where zero is neutral. List them in a spreadsheet as individuals for those close to the project and groups for larger sets of people who can be categorized together (that is, collectively have the same impact). It may be helpful to plot them in a two-by-two matrix with influence on one scale and support on the other. This simple categorization provides insights into how you should engage with them. Highly influential and highly supportive (3, 3) makes a good sponsor and needs to be engaged to leverage their political power. Highly influential people with low or negative support (3, −3) are potential adversaries who need to be managed even more closely to mitigate the damage they may cause. An example of this may be an external protest group or an internal team competing for resources. Neutral on both scales (0, 0) are more passive observers

of your activities. Low influence and high support are enthusiasts or potential advocates, which may represent members of your team or family members. They are good to have as moral support, but are not necessarily able to contribute in tangible ways to your cause.

2. Assess a situation of past experience when the expectations of two stakeholders or groups of stakeholders progressively diverged. Share the story and ask members of your discussion group or team how they would have rectified the situation earlier. Challenge whether you effectively assessed your stakeholders and how well you specifically targeted your communications plans to align with their needs.

3. Gather a diverse group of people in your workplace and ask them to share what they see as examples of good leadership or good management. Write down some key words for their narratives in a column under Leadership or Management (differentiating between failures and successes under each heading). After going through several examples, explore whether there are any commonly occurring themes in any of the four areas. Discuss how these common themes can be rectified, using leadership to seek options and management approaches to implement priority actions informed from this activity.

Additional learning resources:
www.intelligentanswers.com.au/KnowledgeSuccession

CHAPTER 6

Reflective Cycles Are Key to Relevant Capability Development

Executive Summary

Chapter 6 explores how reflection can enable us to be more effective. Not just as the projects proceeds, but also before, during, and after the project. Key points of this chapter are:

- All projects are strategic (otherwise don't do them).
- How the reflective performance cycle aligns behaviors around the conversations being facilitated to leverage behavioral diversity and increase performance.
- Why learning is critical to sustained performance and competitive advantage and how to know if it is happening properly.

Reflective cycles are not practiced enough in many organizations, but are embedded into high-performing organizations, because they value:

1. Why reflection matters;
2. Multiple loop learning; and
3. Feedback and assessment within and of projects.

Why Reflection Matters

Reflection is an interesting word that, like many other words used in this book, has many meanings. In the context of projects and learning, to reflect is to deliberately look closely at the activities being done and assess them to understand them more deeply. Reflection is the active process of critically assessing past, present, and possible future outcomes in order to learn and improves one's capabilities, actions, and decision making.[1] Thinking about what you are doing before acting, as you do it, or after you have done it seems like a sensible process that should always happen, but in practice this does not occur as often as it should. People often act on "gut feel" or "intuition" or assume that because something worked before or in another situation, it is appropriate to repeat it in another context. However, this is fraught with dangers not apparent without reflection. Reflective practice provides a link between theory and practice,[2] in that it operates as an effective tool to transform our tacit knowledge (or should that be perspective?) into a range of options for action, or to understand the limitations of past actions.

Reflective practice, when implemented well, enables us to find evidence, or indicate a lack thereof, to support or reject a path of action. It highlights the potential strengths and weaknesses of our actions so that we have a more successful and sustainable future. Reflection can be done as a self-guided activity, but can be much richer and more insightful when openly engaged with others to reflect on interpretations through different lenses and experiences.[3] Collective reflection can help people clarify and validate their thoughts and emotions and assist them to focus on their development and progress.[4] The ultimate aim of reflective practice is to improve one's professional practice and performance, while also contributing to the improvement of others. Reflective practice is a critical element of many developmental and learning aspects of professional life, and is embedded in decision making, analysis, education, mentoring, coaching, and facilitation processes such as after-action reviews and lessons learned.

Although Donald Schön is often credited with the development of reflective practice, his considerable contributions built on the foundations of John Dewey, who wrote about the need for reflective thinking as early as 1903. Dewey[5] identified the three characteristics or attitudes of people who are reflective as open-mindedness, responsibility, and wholeheartedness,[6] which have been incorporated into developmental activities in other fields and practices.[7] People can reflect to review their practice across three timeframes: past, present, and future. Schön defined the capacity to reflect "on action" and "in action" as core elements of learning in professional practice. My own research[8] explored the benefits of reflection on future-planned actions and aligning behaviors with actions. This allows adjustments to deliver better outcomes and enhances performance over time. Reflecting forward is one of the most powerful things that successful people do. It enables them to more effectively evaluate options through mental simulations and assess the plan against a range of alternative possibilities.

Reflection matters because it makes us better informed about the things that we have done, are doing, and are planning to do. Being a reflective practitioner enables us to accelerate our learning and socialize ideas with others to enhance performance for all involved.

The highest levels of performance come to people who are centered, intuitive, creative and reflective—people who know to see a problem as an opportunity. Deepak Chopra

Multiple Loop Learning

In this book I often refer to iterative loops or cycles. The value of repeated cycles of clarification and exploration are rooted in the multiple-loop learning theory. In fact, this model itself emerged from a number of ideas across different disciplines trying to apply the concepts in practice to understand learning at different levels. Argyris and Schön[9] are generally credited as the founders of the term double-loop learning, but they never discussed triple- or multiple-loop learning specifically. Several other researchers and practitioners quickly adopted the idea of increasing the depth of understanding through questioning at different depths with different focus areas through various multiple loop processes. Although the history of this development has been the topic of some fascinating academic studies (see Chapter 9), it is the practical implications that are most valuable.

I have assimilated some of the important aspects of multiple-loop learning into Figure 6.1. The simplest explanation is this process adjusts the focus of questioning in your reflection practice through the different loops, and this changes the depth of understanding you generate. At the simplest reflection level (loop 1), questions asked reveal the basics of the cause and effect observed: stating the facts of *"this happened because that*

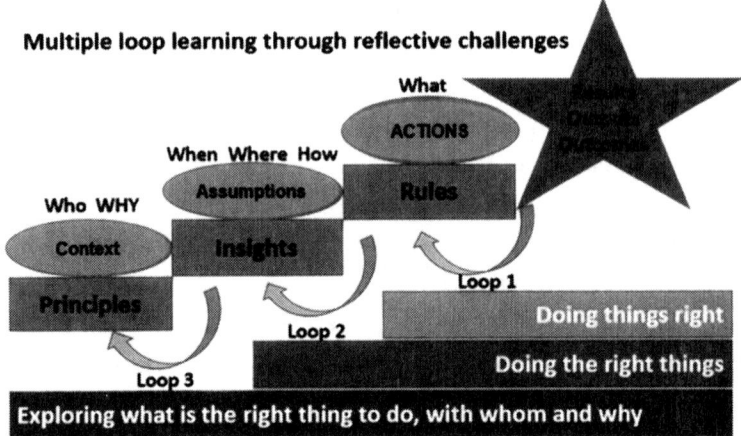

Figure 6.1 *Depth of reflection and purpose for Multiple Loop Learning*

happened." It relates the action (trigger) to the result (outputs and outcomes) in a shallow or rudimentary way. This is very focused on what action was taken and what result occurred: "We achieved budget, that's great, let's celebrate." Or from a failure perspective: "That didn't work, let's avoid doing that ever again." This basic reflection level can be used to establish rules for simple tasks that do not need to change, but has limited effect if changes occur that impact the actions.

Loop 2 takes the understanding of what happened from loop 1 to a deeper level. It starts to examine if this was the right way to approach the actions or questions the timing and place of the actions. It seeks to assess alternatives to what happened or find ways to change the assumptions on which the rules of loop 1 might not be relevant or applicable. Loop 2 looks toward other options that may be better aligned with the desired outcomes or generate superior outputs and considers that circumstances might change. It extends the focus from *what* happened to *when, where,* and *how* alternatives may be created that will provide enhanced performance from the current rules and processes. The dialogue here is: "We achieved budget so far, but we know the economy is moving downward; let's explore what we can control and what alternative markets may be available." Or from a failure perspective: "We need to understand that our offerings are not relevant anymore, so we can get the budget back on track." This more complicated reflection can be used to redraft rules, adjust decision-making approaches, and guide product and service offerings in response to changes.

Loop 3 starts to challenge the current understanding of what is happening and how to explore whether a complete change of direction is appropriate. Everything is reassessed, including the principles upon which people are engaging with each other and whether the contexts they do this in are valid. It is focused on why decisions are taken and seeks to validate current paths or find completely new paths for perhaps different reasons. Loop 3 is the type of thinking that triggers transformational changes such as a complete career path shift or an organization shifting into a completely new market or product and services market. This deepest level of reflection should be practiced when leaders are discussing strategy with an open and challenging mindset that acknowledges changes are a certainty within the longer-term timeframe they are considering. It deepens the focus and at the same time broadens the scope of feeling, thinking, and actions. In this loop, we challenge who we are and why this is important and then create a range of options that we wish to pursue in future. The dialogue here is more exploratory than the higher-level loops and acknowledges a greater level of uncertainty, which requires those in the conversation to revert right back to principles and values: "Why are we proceeding with this path? It seems that the market may be maturing and we need to create a disruptive innovation before a competitor does, or perhaps even shift to a new area of business?" Or from a failure perspective: "Why did we completely miss that shift? We now have to completely rethink why we are in this market and what alternatives there may be for us to recover our sales and reputation." This loop explores the complexities that modern organizations face and provides a foundation to keep performance high by being proactive rather than reactive. Done well, it will enable the organization to remain ahead of the competition and leading the changes. Not done or poorly done, results in them following others and responding to the changes forced upon them by the leaders (who are doing this type of reflection).

Academics continue to argue about who gets credit for what parts of the models and concepts behind multiple-loop learning and whether the philosophical approach is aligned with the theoretical constructs and academic robustness of the theories. Meanwhile, practitioners have embedded the insights into many pragmatic tools and processes to create value. Examples include "The Five Whys" (delving through layers to deeper understanding) and some forms of risk assessment and root cause analysis. The nature of the reflection you do makes a significant difference to the contributions you make to society, discussed in greater detail in Chapter 9.

Feedback and Assessment Within and of Projects

The entire world and everything in it works better when people understand the purpose of feedback. Too often feedback is not well received as it is perceived to be criticism. While this is sometimes the case, even sharp criticism can be extremely useful if we reflect on it in an appropriate way. The challenge is to be able to take in feedback and assess it from your perspective and try to objectively challenge yourself to consider if this is just unjustified emotional complaints or it is in fact a passionate plea to get to you understand something critically important. People disagree all the time. As long as this can be shared and reflected on in a professional manner, benefits can flow from the diversity of opinion. Research on problem-solving scenarios often shows that someone with an excellent suggestion or even the optimal answer can offer it, but their contribution is completely ignored and the activity ends up in failure. Some literature refers to such insights as "outliers"[10] or "weak signals."[11]

Your own body is completely dependent on a myriad of feedback loops. It subconsciously reads temperature, and demand for oxygen and energy, and these measures trigger responses such as perspiration, breathing rate, and heart rate to maintain the optimal performance level, according to the conditions you are in within than moment. Without being able to assimilate all this feedback, your body would not be able to perform as a whole and may even completely stop performing if it cannot respond to the environmental conditions. It is not just physical feedback. Your brain is very actively taking in all types of environmental information through sight, sound, and touch, including reading and interpreting emotions and body language to evoke automated responses. Depending on what the brain perceives the situation to be, it will trigger arousal, and flight or fight responses through the release of a range of bioactive chemicals into your blood or brain. Physiological responses and habits[12] are formed in response to these triggers. These may be beneficial, such as social support and friendships, or detrimental, such as depression or ana- phylaxis. You can, through enhanced emotional intelligence,[13] become more consciously aware of your own emotional signals and why you have your habits. Reflection on these helps you to make better choices than the automated responses, and you can learn to override these to respond better in stressful situations.

In our highly politically and socially correct world, we sometimes become oversensitive to some of these signals, reading more into them than was meant by those transmitting the signals. Overly officious con- trol of social interactions can lead to feedback being totally stopped. This blockage of feedback in organizations and teams can cause extremely neg- ative impacts. It is like completely preventing the body from receiving the signals it needs to remain balanced and maintain the homeostasis essential to good performance. Equally, because the sociopolitical feedback mech- anisms have been blocked, when a signal does come, the organization can completely overreact to it causing an explosion like an anaphylactic shock. In such cases, the reaction becomes more damaging to the culture than the actual danger that triggered the reaction. Overreactions due to overcontrol are becoming more of a problem; overindulgence in poor behavior can also happen due to a fear of providing feedback that may be perceived as negative. The sociopolitical environment in your work- place or project is absolutely critical to its performance, and this needs to be actively discussed and demonstrated through excellent leadership role modeling and mentoring.

There are many excellent ways to constructively solicit professional feedback, and many organizations have processes in place to gather and act on it. Some examples are project reviews, postproject audits, lessons learned, simulations, and simply asking questions. Done well, all of these can provide excellent insights, and done poorly, all can exacerbate difficult situations. It is not the process that is generally the issue: it is whether and how it is done. Intent and behavioral environment are critical to leveraging benefits from these activities, and leaders must clarify what is and is not appropriate in your team. Your team environment is just like your body, in that it needs effective feedback mechanisms to maintain healthy performance. Too little or too much creates imbalance. Both too sensitive and too insensitive cause misunderstandings. Feedback processes are a critical mechanism to ensure balanced performance, whether it be on a momentary, daily, weekly, or less regular basis: in private conversations between individual team members or in whole of team meetings; or before, during, or after the work.

The culture of any organization is shaped by the worst behavior the leader is willing to tolerate.[14]

Contributor Case Study

Bill Kaplan, Working Knowledge, USA

Mid Cap Federal Government Consulting Company

Company Knowledge Challenges Focuses on Performance
   There were four primary knowledge challenges:

1. the explicit or formal management of knowledge in ongoing operations
2. improving the ability to leverage the hidden value of corporate knowledge in business development and new consulting solution creation
3. improving the ability to learn from past failures and successes in strategic decision making and client solution delivery
4. creating value from knowledge, experience, and insight held by both our company employees and clients.

   The Performing and Learning framework adopted by the company required a reflection-based operating model that focused on four essential elements:

1. Learning Processes
2. Communities of Practice (CoP)
3. Knowledge Assets (Core Knowledge Base)
4. Enabling Technology

Element 1—Learning Processes: The learning processes enabled the company to capture knowledge (explicit (codified) and tacit (personal)) and make sense out of it before, during, and after work was done. These processes provided the captured and distillable content for the knowledge assets (knowledge repositories with knowledge artifacts) that were accessible by subject and practice area across the company.

Element 2—CoPs: The company supported two types of CoPs: *organizationally driven and practitioner driven*. Both were voluntary, encouraged, and supported at all levels. Knowledge from conversations in the CoPs were harvested and characterized for reuse in company knowledge assets so that it could be searched, accessed, and adapted for reuse by fellow practitioners within that CoP or within other CoPs (cross-linkage).

Element 3—Knowledge assets (Knowledge repositories): Web based, they contained:

- key insights, learnings, and advice in the form of guidelines, checklists, effective practices, and "first person told stories," often in the form of short video vignettes that clearly highlight critical learnings, insight, or experience
- the business "context" in which the learning occurred
- expertise location
- a link directly to relevant "just-in-time" training.

Element 4—Enabling technology: Enabling technology was the IT infrastructure and applications that enabled "connection, collection, and collaboration" from any location.

To embed the KM Framework and the KM tools and techniques into the fabric of operations, the CKO created two additional roles: Knowledge Engineers (KEs) and Engagement Knowledge Managers (EKMs).

Four Big Lessons from the journey:

1. A shared context.
2. Embedding and integrating a common, simple set of core reflective, capture, transfer, and reuse practices which are easily understood.

3. Knowledge must move within and across the company on two levels, reflective peer to peer transfer of knowledge and continuously characterizing the learning for reuse in the context of the user of the knowledge.

4. This sustainable ability to "connect, collect and collaborate" enabled the company to create the long-term value required for sustained growth and success.

Reflective Activities and Additional Learning Resources for the Curious Executive and Students

Applying this learning in practice

1. Invite a small group of colleagues to discuss how they have used reflection to change their approach in future situations and highlight what the impact implementing this change was for them and others. When the first participant is done, others can constructively challenge by asking question about how they "know" the impact was real—what evidence exists to support perceived benefits. As the conversation slows, another participant who has a natural link to the previous topic can follow with their example to continue the conversation.

2. Use Figure 6.1 to think about how often you invest time at each of the three levels of learning and what the impacts of this are. Too much or too little time in each layer can lead to problems, as all are relevant to overall performance. Write a paragraph on an instance when you successfully learned and changed your approach as a result and another when you did not get this right. Share this with a colleague and ask for their feedback.

3. Arrange a regular feedback meeting to practice providing and receiving feedback. Ensure that the process is done in an appropriate manner. Aim to achieve the "Goldilocks Approach": not too hot, not too cold—just right. The more your team practices giving and receiving constructive feedback, the greater the trust will build. Once you have

an environment of growing trust, collaboration increases, knowledge is shared, which generates more new knowledge and performance increases. The better you get at this, the less stressful and more engaged your team and the more positive your workplace relationships become!

Additional learning resources:

www.intelligentanswers.com.au/KnowledgeSuccession

CHAPTER 7

Creative Friction Through Conversations

Executive Summary

Chapter 7 reveals that the majority of knowledge created in projects is tacit in nature and is generated in social interactions. We explore why conversation is critical to build trust and enable the flow of knowledge. This discussion also highlights how a lack of appropriate conversations blocks knowledge flow and causes tension among the stakeholders. Key points of this chapter are:

- Conversation is underestimated as a business tool and poorly used in many organizational environments.
- Using the art of persuasion to positively influence, rather than manipulate.
- Learning how to develop more effective facilitation capabilities.

Conversation, and therefore knowledge co-creation, can be more effectively created through attention to the following four concepts:

1. Great ideas are stimulated and nurtured from insights;
2. The structure of "Conversations that Matter";
3. Facilitating effective interactions; and
4. Elevating participation.

Great Ideas Are Stimulated and Nurtured from Insights

Earlier in this book I mentioned insights from Stephen Johnson's *Where Do Good Ideas Come From* and also Gary Klein's *Seeing What Others Don't*. Both of these books explore how people engage in conversations to explore new possibilities. Connecting these two books, we can see that collective co-creation of ideas is a very social activity. Both creating ideas and nurturing these into implementable projects to generate products and services benefits from including a diversity of perspectives and iterative reflective cycles. During my three decades of exploring a wide range of books about the source of ideas, working in product development, delivering international projects, and asking experts what is important, I realized that creating and nurturing ideas requires many reflective processes and significant passion and persistence. Klein highlighted that the stereotypical image of an independent genius suddenly creating a magical moment to produce a stunning idea is a rarity. The best ideas emerge from a range of stimuli that trigger a unique set of circumstances or need. Klein suggested the insights can be triggered through creative desperation, connections, or leveraging contradictions. While increasing creativity certainly stimulates more ideas, the idea is just the beginning of the project. Maintaining creativity for analysis and problem solving during the subsequent projects makes the whole process more effective and efficient. Someone has to care enough about the idea and engage people around it and nurture it through its early days, where it may easily fall prey to the powerful forces of "status quo maintenance" and "not invented here."

Momentum is a powerful factor that keeps organizations and economies flowing in a steadily controlled and predictable path. Huge investments in current momentum lead to great resistance to change by those who have made those investments. The more divergent the new idea is from the current direction, the more likely those presently in power will want to crush it—unless they can see that it increases their benefit and influence. Change introduces uncertainty and risk to the understood status quo. Many large companies have a strategy of buying out smaller organizations before they become a potential competitor. While some organizations integrate the new idea into their own products and services, more often they implement buy-outs as a risk mitigation activity that keeps the commercial landscape clean. It is like weeding a garden so that only those plants you specifically planted are displayed. A seed floating in from elsewhere is usually not welcomed and must be quickly removed before it becomes a pest.

Google's 20 percent discretionary time[1] for exploring other projects has generated many ideas to grow the scope of Google's activities. However, many of the ideas from this program are spun off as start-ups so that Google can control this breadth of activity and maintain focus. The program enables a diversity of ideas to be developed to a reasonable degree of maturity, which are then culled back to the ideas most aligned with the core momentum of the organization. The essential insights of this program is both divergence of new ideas and convergence of the best ideas must be fostered to stimulate innovation. It also leverages the personal passions of employees by allowing them to invest in their own pet projects, which excites and engages knowledge workers. The outcomes are very different from telling people what projects they must work on and tightly controlling their access resources.

Creative Friction accelerates the rate and quality of ideas generated by proactively and constructively criticizing ideas. The simplest definition of Creative Friction is *fostering an environment in which people proactively challenge each other's contributions in a constructive way to achieve performance improvements.* Metaphorically, Creative Friction is a mental arm wrestle exercise designed to strengthen the arms of both participants. Professional critical challenges, which highlight possibilities for improvement, stimulate development of concepts to make them more robust. We invest effort to understand one another and stimulate a mindset of positively adopting feedback. Under these circumstances, gathering disparate groups of people creates a diverse environment where concepts can be discussed from a variety of perspectives. Getting participants to acknowledge their differences and provide permission to disagree provides the right environment to foster constructive exchange. Committing to listen in a nondefensive way to open conversation can stimulate rich reflective exchanges that generate insights.

The adage that *everything that does not kill us makes us stronger* is adopted in an environment where criticism does not disparage the idea, but instead highlights potential opportunities to extend the idea and mitigate against weaknesses. This is a slight variation of the Creative Abrasion process described by Dorothy Leonard.[2] However, the process itself is not what brings the creativity. The creativity comes from how the facilitator leads the environment to keep everyone involved and draw the full diversity of concepts from the room. Leonard, and others since, have successfully combined creativity and cycles of divergent and convergent conversation to help productivity in a range of situations and organizations. The essence of success is to ensure that the participants are aligned in their thinking in the moment and this thinking is aligned with the purpose of that particular conversation. This concept of parallel thinking was developed in Edward de Bono's highly successful "Six Hats" method.[3] My own research extended this idea to combine reflective practice, conversation structure, and behavioral environment to achieve better outcomes, the foundation of which is the "Conversations That Matter" approach as described as follows.

The Structure of "Conversations That Matter"

A "Conversation That Matters" is an exchange of ideas to understand the optimal next steps for any given situation. Such conversations are consciously structured in a particular way and have a particular purpose as shown in Figure 7.1. They are best done with some planned structure and understanding of desired outcomes, although not performed with so much rigidity that they do not allow the emergence of new ideas and concepts. The first element of a conversation that matters is for all involved to understand the purpose of the conversation and to align their thinking and behavior to achieve this. Facilitated well, conversations that matter lead to progress on four key elements: tangible outputs, intangible

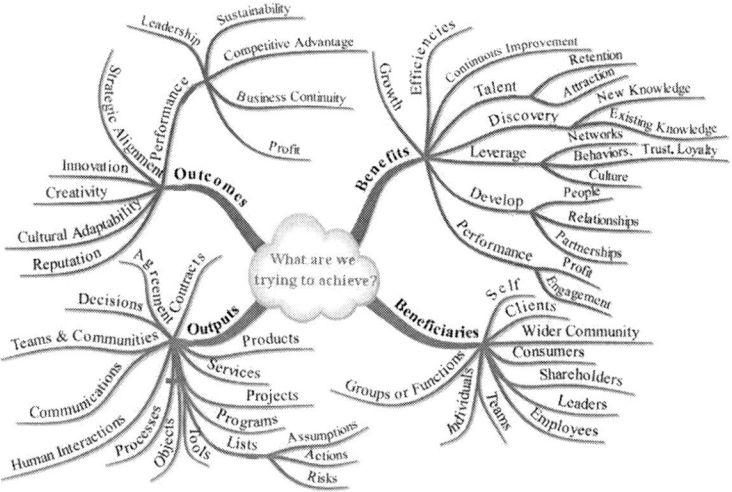

Figure 7.1 Conversations that matter: The structure of effective dialogue

outcomes, benefits, and beneficiaries. Before discussing these elements in detail, let's explore a slightly wider topic of conversation to set the context.

Conversations are interesting. We have them all the time, often without thinking too much about what it is we want to talk about. Sometimes we reflect upon them in great depth and at other times they simply happen and are not contemplated again. Many conversations are quite informal, though they can be formal, such as the performance appraisals done regularly by many organizations. Informal conversations embrace nearly any topic to socialize and connect people and maintain friendships, whereas formal conversations are usually around structured topics such as contractual obligations, legal implications, project status, or role expectations. While most conversations are face to face between two or more people, in our modern world, they can include a wide range of other options. Examples include virtual interactions through videoconference, e-mail, or social media or even a reflective conversation with oneself. Regardless of their specific purpose, conversations are a fundamental tool through which people engage in a dialogue of thoughts and ideas for a wide range of purposes. The importance of conversation is demonstrated by the fact that most people want to engage with another person before making any significant decision. *iKNOW* Magazine published an entire edition dedicated to conversation and its impacts.[4]

People easily engage in general chatter that is politically and socially safe, but will usually prefer to avoid controversial topics that cause robust debate. Stimulating conversations that matter around such topics can be highly rewarding, but are more challenging. This is especially true if trust is low or relationships are weak among the people involved. Discussing sensitive topics can involve exchanging views and opinions that are contradictory. These pose significant risks of conflict if not managed well. Exchanging views on passions, political differences, and emotional perspectives is useful, but can also lead group interactions toward messy and uncomfortable states. The challenges of facilitating such interactions is often considered too difficult for many people, especially for inexperienced managers. Naïve initiation can sometimes find the inexperienced facilitator quickly out of their depth in an uncontrolled, escalating crisis. Uncontrolled conversations can cause significant damage to relationships and limit the willingness to share knowledge or participate in future interactions. However, with the right mindset, facilitation and open approach, courageous conversations around difficult issues and opportunities can be extremely productive for the individuals and groups involved. They can stimulate significant contributions to the wider organization or community. Competent leaders create a safe environment to debate a potentially unsafe topic, and this can defuse potential issues before they irreversibly damage relationships.

> *The kind of conversation I like is one in which you are prepared to emerge a slightly different person.*
>
> —Theodore Zeldin

A little preparation for a conversation goes a long way toward more effective results. After establishing the purpose of the conversation among participants, a quick verification of the element(s) (output, outcome, benefits, and beneficiaries) this conversation focuses the attention and dialogue on the priority. A conversation can work through all four in order to make sure the elements are adequately covered. See Figure 7.1 for more detailed, but not exclusive, list of options.

- **What are we trying to achieve?**
  To engage in optimal conversations that matter, all involved
  must agree what they are discussing and how they would
  describe it in each of the following elements. This clarity
  of purpose sets the context of the conversation and enables
  aligned thinking and behavior. Such alignment is important
  because conversations like brainstorming creative divergent
  thinking aligned with engaging behaviors generate the best
  results (e.g., de Bono's green and yellow hats with Organizational Zoo's Eagle, Bee, and Owl). However, this approach
  would be ineffective for a prioritization conversation, where
  analytical thinking and constructively critical behaviors would
  be more appropriate (e.g., de Bono's black hat with Organizational Zoo's combination of Lion and Vulture). Open
  discussion of these approaches leads to better engagement of
  ideas and fewer misunderstandings and better performance.
- **What tangible outputs will be generated?**
  Outputs are sharable quantifiable objects, usually immediately
  available and often short term and tactical in nature. For a
  brainstorming (divergent) conversation, the output will be a
  list of options. For a prioritization (convergent) conversation,
  the list from the brainstorming will be reduced to a few ideas
  as foundations for projects. An output could be something as
  significant as a signature for financial support or it could be a
  wide range of less significant results such as an agreement in
  principle, or permission to explore an option further to determine if it should be committed to at a later time.
- **What intangible outcomes will be created?**
  Outcomes are more difficult to define precisely than outputs,
  making them more difficult to describe accurately and share.
  They are usually more long term and strategic in nature and
  include emotional or cultural impacts. For a brainstorming
  conversation, the outcomes could be that we had a lot of fun
  and generated a great deal of trust. Measuring this is difficult,
  but participants can feel whether this was true, or the opposite occurred. People not present find it hard to know because

they did not experience the conversation, and it is a challenge for them to know exactly what it was like, or if shared descriptions of it were accurate. For an effective prioritization conversation, the outcome may be a high level of confidence in the new way forward. Equally, it could be a significant conflict that will undermine harmony if not well facilitated.

- **What benefits will be achieved?**
  The right-hand side of the conversations that matter structure (Benefits and Beneficiaries) to some extent focuses on the positive aspects of the left-hand side (Outputs and Outcomes). They focus on the specific impacts that will be achieved. Benefits can still be intangible or tangible, but the difference in this side is the specific details of who gets what from the conversation. Some conversations are about benefits to those in the conversations, such as a board discussing their own fees. The same board could make a decision to act to increase the confidence (intangible benefit) for investors (external beneficiaries). A charitable organization could be engaging potential donors (external stakeholders who get intangible benefits of knowing they are making a difference) to make donations (tangible output) so that an underprivileged community (external beneficiaries) can reduce poverty or infant morbidity (tangible benefits). The precise categorization of the elements is less important that ensuring the conversation is proactively considering WHY this conversation is important.

- **Who will be the beneficiaries?**
  As discussed before, this describes who gets the benefits. This may be a specific person, organization, or community or it could be a benefit for the common good. The beneficiaries of a conversation may not always be immediately apparent. Sometimes they are the focus of the conversation and the reason for it and on other occasions they could be serendipitous beneficiaries not considered in the conversation, especially if the conversation was not well facilitated or did not occur before an action was taken. Facilitating conversations that matter in advance of decisions not only considers all

beneficiaries of decision and actions, but also considers who may be adversely impacted by it. It is rare for actions to be beneficial to every stakeholder group, so we must understand the negative consequences for other stakeholder groups and if and how adversely affected groups need to be compensated.

A quick validation of the conversation can be achieved by asking these questions again at the end. This should ensure the conversation optimizes the return on the time and effort invested. Highlighting each of the five elements after the conversation means all participants leave the conversation with a common understanding of why this conversation mattered.

Creating the right environment for a conversation that matters varies for different cultures and groups. In stereotypical Western cultures, a more open exploratory approach is easier to achieve, but this can be more challenging in a stereotypical Eastern culture. Relationships and hierarchy sensitivities impact what can be said and how it is stated. It is critical to understand the cultural norms and work within the environment in which you are operating, including social connection networks and political alliances. Attempts to drive conversations that ignore important cultural aspects will fail, and participation in subsequent sessions will be low. A statement that is considered direct but acceptable in one culture can be viewed as rude, impertinent, or completely unacceptable in another. The optimal approach to facilitating conversations that matter is to invest heavily in planning before the conversation. Talk with a range of potential participants one to one and ask them for their advice on a range of possible outcomes. Listen first and then explore with open questions. Invite them to participate with statements they are comfortable with and ask them how they would like to be engaged. You are more likely to achieve your desired outcomes when the participants have been preinformed of the situations and they understand why it is good for them to support your recommendations. Some consider this the normal and courteous approach to influence, others see it as manipulative. Stakeholder perspective is critical to what can be achieved in conversations. This is discussed more thoroughly in Chapter 12.

Two-way conversations are valid for all contexts and essential in situations of leadership, mentoring, coaching, and counseling. Some examples of important organizational and project conversations that matter are strategy reviews, after-action reviews, lessons learned, problem solving, risk assessment, providing feedback, succession planning, performance reviews, induction of new employees, community of practice outcomes, organizational culture, and values and behavioral expectations. All of these topics need discussion to generate a more productive environment, reduce risks, optimize learning, and to maximize conversion of potential into value. Stimulating conversations between people who should be interacting with each other is a significant part of successful leadership and management. These conversations can build relationships, encourage innovation, trigger stories, share knowledge, and highlight or resolve previously unforeseen opportunities, risks, and issues. Facilitating a conversation that matters is as much an art as a science. Understanding what role to play, and when to switch, that takes time to perfect. How effectively the facilitator of the conversations switches between these roles and adapts their behavior is a significant factor in determining the outcome.

Facilitating Effective Interactions

The best conversations are social, experiential, and developmental. Such interactions lead to mutually agreed actions. They engage participants in an open exchange of perspectives through which all involved become more informed. This generates both enhanced relationships and leads to social interaction. Such outcomes are not achieved by accident; they occur with careful planning and with a deep understanding of the values, cultural norms, behaviors, and expectations of the stakeholders involved. As with most situations, there is a fine line between disaster and success. Every problem is an opportunity to act to create value, and every opportunity has significant risks, which can lead to irreparable damage, both tangible and intangible. This is exactly why conversations are important. They offer the opportunity to gather other's perspectives of the risk-to-benefit ratio and listen to alternative approaches for success. The more perspectives you are aware of, the more you can leverage to achieve the benefits and mitigate the risks. As you experience conversations and reflect on the effectiveness of successes and failures, you increase your knowledge and understanding of how to leverage the diversity. This in turn will elevate your confidence, which inspires confidence in others. This iterative evolution creates a master facilitator and gradually increases your ability and effectiveness to make a significant sustainable difference.

Presenters often apologize when they share a complex, messy, or busy PowerPoint slide. They assume that the audience cannot comprehend anything with more than six bullet points. If you need the complexity to explain the concept you wish to share—don't apologize, explain. If you don't need the detail in the slide, take it out and only share what is needed to make the point without apologies. Adding more or less than you need only distracts the attention of the audience. Slides should not be about "content" to complete a conversation; they should provoke questions so the audience engages in conversations, verbal or self-reflective, depending on the situation. Presenters achieve better outcomes if they stimulate a reflective conversation that matters with a trusted other, or even with themselves, to determine what they are trying to achieve before designing a presentation.

What information is essential to inform a target audience is one of the biggest challenges faced by educators, leaders, coaches, and mentors (and I would argue parents)? That is, how to fully inform and motivate those you are trying to help. You want them to immerse themselves in the topic, so they deeply understand it. The best learners, mentees, and students read everything you provide, engage in deep conversations by sharing their own insights and experiences, and provide reflective comments and feedback to others. However, these are the natural lifelong learners that every leader, mentor, and coach dreams of. Stereotypically, and perhaps somewhat harshly, students in formal studies are often perceived to want to know just enough to obtain the qualifications. Often they seem spread between too many priorities. They simply don't have the time to know everything they need to know (but, of course, still may have an expectation of a high grade). Whose responsibility is it to ensure that your target audience (whether they be followers of you as a leader, your students, mentees, or perhaps employees across a large organization) is engaged? Too often, each party blames the other in this complex relationship.

To engage people to participate effectively, first ask yourself: Why should anyone listen to you or be led by you?[5] Hopefully, they will reflect on the same question. Smart people are inspired by reputation and achievement, which is very different from fame and celebrity. When they find good reasons, they will follow. As stated elsewhere in this book, genuine leaders have willing intelligent followers. In my opinion, a leader's most important role is to develop others capable of replacing them and supporting them to extend sustainable benefits for the wider community. Sadly, this more philanthropic concept of leadership has diminished. Leadership role models are now more about the personality, charisma, and popularity of the incumbent, than respect for the role being filled and its community impact. The idea that humility is the ultimate characteristic of great leaders[6] has been lost, as many modern leaders focus more on self and short-term thinking, a trend that we can hopefully reverse. The many abridged versions of this book are testimony to the modern rushed approach. People just want the essence of the message and are not prepared to invest the time to read and digest the deeper insights in the original. Fortunately, the principles of servant leadership[7] survive. Genuine leaders who believe in these do practice them, but they do not receive mass acknowledgment, nor do they seek it. If you genuinely want to facilitate engaging participation, read some of the texts described in this section, find a mentor who lives by them, learn how to do this yourself as quickly as you can, and start practicing!

How do we create the environment where people want to continue to engage in their own development so that they can become effective leaders? Variety of roles is good and lifelong learning is essential. However, diversity of experiences and continuity of development must also be balanced. Dorothy Leonard highlighted that it takes on average seven years[8] of full-time work in a given field to become a genuine expert. How can this be achieved when people on average are changing not just roles, but organizations and industries several times within this period? What level of knowledge and skill can we reasonably expect a student emerging from a postgraduate program to have? Answers vary enormously. Ultimately, which answer sits most comfortably comes back to having the right conversation about the expected learning outcomes for the activity. Will the students be experts upon graduating? Are they adequately knowledgeable to deliver basic or advanced tasks in the profession? Can they just describe a theory on their area of study, or can they adeptly apply the relevant aspects of the theories in practice? The optimal way to explore all these questions is to start a Conversation That Matters by asking the foundational question: *What are we trying to achieve?*

Personally, I'm always ready to learn, although I do not always like being taught.

—Winston Churchill

Elevating Participation

How do you get people to engage in your Conversations That Matter? The simplest response to this is have something worthwhile to talk about and make the interaction interesting for all involved. A more meandering and creative exploration of this question follows.

People are now so busy that they are often completely focused on their own goals, largely because they are measured and rewarded on how well these are delivered. A common issue is they assume that any talk is a distraction from their goals and objectives. We all learned this from the traditional education system where students in school were punished for talking, rather than listening to the teacher. Traditionally, the teacher was considered the font of all the knowledge and the students were expected to listen, remember, and recite back the facts of the matter to demonstrate they had "learned." The focus was on content and known information and often devoid of any context the learner could relate it to. Learners were very often able to describe or list the facts, but not necessarily to apply them, or help to resolve an unfamiliar challenge. While this may be a good outcome for "the system" and is an efficient way to deliver known knowledge, standardized people who color between the lines and use the same formula to calculate life's answers can produce poor outcomes for humanity.[9] We all benefit when our next generation is fully engaged in asking challenging questions and looking to explore options, rather than simply finding the known solution, although both are important.

Children naturally understand that "learning by doing" is the optimal way to learn. They play and experiment, despite not understanding the eclectic path they are treading. They do it because it works. Then education seeks to create rules to mold our citizens into a desired type, which ultimately reduces diversity and stifles creativity. Babies are a good example of learning by doing as they experience what is around them through all senses: touch, sight, smell, and especially hearing and taste. Give a baby something unfamiliar and their natural curiosity will trigger them to immediately shake it and bring it to their mouth to get a sense of what it is. Starting with sound (does it rattle, crinkle, or clunk) and rapidly progressing to taste, touch, sight, and smell; babies use their senses to absorb all information they can extract about the object. They explore it from all perspectives to make sense of it and determine if they might be able to do something with it. Noiseless and tasteless objects are soon discarded. Dull, colorless objects are passed over for things that are more interesting and can be played with in creative ways. While I do not suggest that one should lick and sniff your teachers to learn, multisensory learning[10] experiences have been shown to be more memorable and powerful than the bland ways a lot of education is delivered. Optimal learning engages participants and brings out their inner child, and this is what your meetings and team interactions should be like. Get this right and people will be asking when your next event is happening. Eager participants will engage in conversations that matter to generate a flow of exciting ideas and fuel innovation. Follow the traditional agenda and don't be surprised when people are too busy to attend, effectively stating they have determined another activity to be more important.

Benjamin Bloom discussed how education experiences occur at different layers. Traditional schooling methods are targeted at knowledge acquisition, the lowest form of learning. This is just the baseline for genuine higher-quality learning. To truly learn about something, the learning experiences (plural as they work best as iterative cycles) need to progress from remembering knowledge through a series of higher-order thinking processes. Although Bloom's hierarchy[11] has been criticized by some, it has strong and widespread acceptance and has evolved to become: Remember (describe knowledge), Understand (explain comprehension), Apply (leverage skills), Analyze (research and assess existing options), Evaluate (make judgments on options), and Create (make new ideas and develop new concepts informed from synergies between prior insights and experiences). This is the cycle every person benefits from using whenever they are confronted with an unfamiliar challenge. It requires a curious mindset and the courage to work outside our comfort zone to bring elements of new ideas together without fear of failure. Each project you face, each unpredicted event in your life, and each new person you meet presents opportunities to develop yourself and co-create something new. However, our patterned and procedural-based traditional education can get in the way of these opportunities. Instead of engaging in exploratory conversations that matter, our learned approach is to focus on "the known facts" and work within our familiar patterns, which inevitably just maintains the status quo.

Fortunately, some advanced educational institutions are changing this traditional approach to education and starting to explore with alternative approaches. Slowly, more socialization of concepts is being practiced and assessments are based on what new ideas students create and how plausible they are. These learning experiences are making a significant difference for the participants involved and generating ongoing positive outcomes. One challenge to be kept in mind is how self-justification of recommended options is a potentially dangerous path. Seeking a diversity of alternative perspectives is a good safety net to challenge your thinking before influencing others. Ego has a stronger influence on your thinking[12] than you may consciously be aware of, a topic we discuss further in Chapter 12.

> It is amazing what you can accomplish if you do not care who gets the credit.
>
> —Harry S. Truman

It is very challenging to maintain sufficient mindshare among leaders: That is, keeping your ideas and projects in their active thinking processes, especially in geographically dispersed teams largely communicating through virtual tools. There are so many projects, causes and activities, and conditions worthy of support, that to get and keep attention/actions requires something special. In an immediacy-based world fueled by social media, initial motivation to engage and maintain ongoing interest and support is difficult. The challenging question is how to gain share of mind for long enough to secure support and amplify your impact in a short-term celebrity-dominated social environment? How do you shift the attention from what someone famous said yesterday, to respect for insights of your own internal informed resources that care about the outcomes and understand the nuances? Even when you secure initial commitment, attention can still quickly shift. People are so busy interacting at a shallow level that they don't have the time to actually take meaningful actions. While it may be briefly emotionally supportive to "like" something on social media, or give a patronizing approval, it takes more practical and visible support to help people get significant projects delivered. Emotional support is important throughout the process, but alone is insufficient to deliver concrete value.

Although it is difficult to change habits,[13] it is possible to engage people in new experiences and in ways that stimulate their interest and still add great value. In some ways it is like neuroplasticity, which enables brains to make new connections to create new patterns when a brain is damaged. If people with damaged brains can learn new and different ways to approach challenges, why don't we learn to proactively do this with fully capable, healthy brains? Of course, we can achieve this! It just requires us to challenge the current norms in constructive ways. That is, generate some creative friction.

Good management is the art of making problems so interesting and their solutions so constructive that everyone wants to get to work and deal with them.

—Paul Hawken

Contributor Case Study

Keith De La Rue, Acknowledge Consulting, Australia

Creative Friction Through Conversations; Casual Discovery

A few years ago, I was working as team leader of a Knowledge Management team in a large Australian company in Melbourne. My team was one of a number of small teams in a Sales Support group, with a head office in Sydney. The group staff and the team leaders were distributed across the two cities, with each team leader managing staff in both cities. At one point, it came to my attention that the team leaders in the Sydney office had developed an opinion that the Melbourne office had become dysfunctional, with low morale and poor performance.

It was evident that there was little discussion across team boundaries, and that staff working remotely from their team leaders suffered from a feeling of disconnection. This led to duplication of effort across the group. I decided to address this by using a technique I had learned from my team leader in a previous role. Once a fortnight, I took all the group staff from the Melbourne office, along with the other local team leaders, to a coffee shop over the road for a one-hour "meeting." The unwritten agenda for this meeting had two very simple items: one—have a chat over a coffee; two—each person to take turns telling the group what they were working over the previous two weeks. The first of these items intentionally occupied more than half of the meeting.

Over the first few meetings, there were several occasions when members of one team found out that a member of another team was working on a related project, but that they previously had no idea of this. Some also expressed difficulty with certain projects, and others offered assistance with these. After several meetings, team morale improved visibly, and there was greatly improved communication across the teams in Melbourne, as well as improved work output and reduced duplication.

At this point, the Sydney-based team leaders had started to notice a change, and wanted to find out about the apparently miraculous transformation in our office. When told how simple it was, they were somewhat incredulous, and some had to come down to see these meetings for themselves. Some who came along to a meeting still had some incredulity. They asked to see the agenda for the meeting, and some wanted to take control of the meeting and introduce some "real" agenda items, such as delivering management reports or other formal presentations. I usually managed to gently dissuade them of this.

The power of these conversations was in the informality itself. While formal agendas may seem very attractive to some, we already had more than enough official management meetings. The casual setting of these meetings made the needed open conversation possible.

In an informal environment outside the office, there was no stigma attached to revealing that you needed help on a project, or that you had just spent the past two weeks working on something that somebody else in another team had the knowledge and resources to have completed in one day.

There can be power in serendipitous "water cooler" conversations, but positive outcomes from such random conversations may not provide reliable or repeatable business benefits. Scheduling regular casual discovery conversations can produce more consistent—and enjoyable—results, enabling more effective teamwork and a more positive work environment.

Reflective Activities and Additional Learning Resources for the Curious Executive and Students

Applying this learning in practice

1. Invite a small group to discuss the structure of Conversations That Matter. Walk through the structure to highlight examples of where your team or organization is effective or ineffective in parts of the structure and what the consequences of this are. Share success and failure stories of when conversations were well or poorly facilitated and why. Explore alternative ways they could have been done.

2. Proactively think about your interactions and the conversations they involve. In particular, assess how well your team and organization reacts to Creative Friction? Consider how consciously constructive feedback is solicited. How effectively is this designed and embedded into interactions and facilitated to achieve desired results? Are the structure and purpose of your key interactions proactively discussed and shared before they happen and are conversations after them reflective? Plan your next interaction in this way and share the outcome with your colleagues (or engage with us at IntelligentAnswers. com.au in a Conversation That Matters).

3. Think about the leadership styles in your workplace and the impact they have on your own level of engagement and participation. Do

they actively ask for critical feedback and, if so, how do they cope with Creative Friction? Have a Conversation That Matters with some colleagues to exchange views on this and see how diverse your perspectives are. Explore the reasons for similarities and differences. What will you try to change as a result?

4. Challenge yourself with the following: Will you plan your conversations and other interactions more before you engage in them? Will you invest more time to engage in deeper conversations and challenge your own patterns of thinking and behavior more robustly? Are there behaviors that you can observe in others that you admire and would like to adopt? Do you have a mentor and, if not, who do you respect and why? Consider how you can engage them to become your mentor and act on it.

Additional learning resources:
www.intelligentanswers.com.au/KnowledgeSuccession

CHAPTER 8

Language and Tools for Efficiency and Effectiveness

Executive Summary

Chapter 8 clears up some of the most common misunderstandings and how these are caused because we assume what is meant and perceive situations, rather than fully understand them. Key points of this chapter are:

- The language of the project environment is misunderstood and this creates errors.
- Understanding some key terms helps focus the conversations and interactions.
- Ensuring teams speak the same language leads to more effective communication.

Language gets insufficient thought and tools get too much focus in modern organizations. We benefit when we are clear about what we are describing and when we use tools to support efficiency and effectiveness rather than focus on the tools themselves. Just as a map or model is not the reality, the tool is not the reason we act. Clarifying some of the terminology, especially around tools and their use, assists us to align our conversations (or ensures we are even having the same conversation).

The following key examples help us to understand why clarity of terminology is essential.

1. Capability AND Capacity.
2. Efficiency AND Effectiveness.
3. Outputs AND Outcomes.
4. Tactics AND Strategy.
5. Metaphor, Symbolism, Humor, AND Political Correctness.

Before we start exploring these specific examples, it is worth considering the impact of language generally. Language is such an important aspect of human communication that we cannot function in modern organizations or societies without it. It can both enable communication and obstruct it. Communicating with someone who does not understand your own native written or spoken language is challenging enough, but even when you speak the same language errors of understanding happen. It is not just the words that carry meaning; it is the context, symbolism, metaphors, tone, body language, and perceived intent that influence how what is said or written is interpreted. Two people can watch and hear exactly the same thing and one is horrified, while the other is amused. This is not necessarily because one has impeccable professional manners and the other doesn't, but because of how they interpret it. Variation in interpretation can be the cause of great conflict, but can also in the right environment be the stimulus for creativity and learning. Clarifying language to understand each other is an important professional skill that is often lacking, replaced by assumptions that others know what we mean and that they would see it as we do. This is rarely true and even more rarely tested to verify understanding.

Many words have a "reputation" and this varies with culture and demographics. What I mean is the same word may carry a completely different meaning among different people because of the way it is used by that particular group, sector, or even country. Words even change in their meaning over time. This is neither right nor wrong; it simply reflects the natural evolution of languages. New words are invented and older words are adapted or adopted for a different purpose either by all or by a particular section of society. The outcome of this is often confusion, or even conflict and people misunderstand what the person they are communicating with. A good example of this the word "gay," which originally meant happy and was even a common name for females. Somewhere, somehow it was adopted to mean homosexual. Dictionary.com lists the modern use of gay as the current accepted sexual preference and then also lists two slang definition and three "older usage" definitions. This change is quite clear to most people, but the nuances of the multiple personalities of some words are not. It is no surprise that people get confused: Even more so when they do not share the same first language and culture. A humorous cross-cultural example is the word "thong." In some societies this traditionally referred to informal cheap footwear, but has become more globally known as a form of underwear. For Australians, in particular, thongs on their feet are just a normal part of informal attire. However, they have become accustomed to being misunderstood when they openly state they are wearing thongs when talking with international visitors.

Another very often misunderstood word is "manipulate." In engineering terms, this word simply means to move, and special tools are designed to manipulate specific machinery parts or objects to get positive outcomes. However, in common global human resources circles, to manipulate is seen as a negative way to influence people. "Politics" is usually seen as a negative word. However, without politically engaging to influence others, we limit what we can achieve. Politics is perceived as manipulative and negative, and this can be the case, but engaging politically can also achieve positive outcomes. It depends on why you do this and how you go about it. How you feel about the political influences depends on your perspective, which is interpreted based on the impact this has on you and your past experiences. Many more words have seemingly opposite, or at least very different, interpretations. You can explore these for your own context in the activities at the end of the chapter.

These last few sentences were added to highlight just how easy it is to think you know what is being stated when in fact you may be completely mistaken. Clarification of intent and meaning is critical to effective communication and is best done by paraphrasing back what you believe was meant. Words are extremely powerful when they are fully understood and potentially extremely destructive if they are not. Misrepresentation of words, such as quoting out of context, is a common way to undermine an enemy. Words have been powerfully used as propaganda. The best speeches have been carefully crafted so that every word has been placed to achieve the most impact. Words can be more powerful than the sword. When applied effectively, words can move nations and inspire others to greatness. Equally, they can cause destruction and conflict.

Continuing with the theme that the world is paradoxical, I have emphasized that it is not one or the other definition that is right in the following pairs of words. The irony is that the words listed are often used and interpreted as the same thing by different people in the same conversation, when in fact they were meaning quite different things without knowing. That said, both of the example words in each case are required for optimal performance. The fact that half the readers will disagree with the definitions I have used here simply reinforces the point I am making. It does not matter if they use other definitions (or is that interpretations?). The important thing is to be clear about exactly what they mean when they use it. I have used the standard dictionary definitions of the words, rather than the common colloquial or jargonistic uses, to highlight the potential for misunderstanding, instead of arguing what the "right" definition is. The right definition is the one that is understood in the same way for everyone in the conversation, as well as by others who may read or hear the conversation later.

Capability AND Capacity

Capability and capacity are the most commonly confused word in organizations. They are very often used interchangeably, but they can mean very different things. The Oxford Dictionary defines "capability" using terms like ability, fitness, power, or faculty. It reflects having the necessary skills and competencies to perform an act or deliver to a standard. Oxford defines "capacity" using volume-related terms such as cubic content, function, or to receive or contain. By these definitions, both capability and capacity are important in workplaces and projects. It is essential not only to build the capability (competency, knowledge, fitness, and faculty) of your resources, but also to have the capacity (volume and content) of resources to be able to deliver outputs and outcomes within the time-frames required. A common error made by managers is basing plans on what they have the capability to do, but ignoring how much capacity they have for this. For example, an organization may have a capable project manager, but that does not mean that this person has the capacity to manage many significant projects at the same time. Poor planning of capabilities or capacities creates unreasonable expectations about delivering and realizing benefits. Think about capability as being what ability or competency you have, and capacity as the level of these resources you have to deliver within the planned timeframes. Capability is a development challenge and relates to the knowledge, skills, and experience levels of the people an organization has access to. Capacity is a prioritization challenge that relates to the availability of these resources when they are needed. Both can be supplemented by outsourcing. However, outsourcing capability creates knowledge issues and risks in the long term that outsourcing capacity usually does not.

In organizational planning contexts, we must have robust conversations about both capabilities and capacities. Projects need the appropriate capacity of the appropriate capabilities at the right phase of a project. Effective planning is not just about how many: It is about how many of what capabilities. Resource planning that simply assumes the competencies, skills, and behaviors of one individual are equivalent to another is destined for failure. Consider your worst educational experience. Compare the value of your learning experience when engaged by your most inspirational teacher with that of the most boring. They both had the same capacity (time), but very different capabilities.

Efficiency AND Effectiveness

These two are less commonly confused, but still occasionally one is used when a person means the other. Efficiency is about accomplishing something with the least waste of resources: That is, delivery of the output with a minimum expenditure of time and effort. Thus, efficiency is a measure of return on effort expended. The bigger the return for a given effort, the greater the efficiency. In common use, "efficient" is often focused on reducing financial or production costs to maximize output (although when taken too far to reap short-term benefits can damage effectiveness of longer-term outcomes). The equivalent engineering terminology is the ratio of the energy developed by a machine to the energy supplied to it. This relationship between input and output is an important consideration that can be expressed as a normal curve. There is an optimal level where inputs and outputs provide highly efficient organizations or team, but too little or too much focus on efficiency can make the organization sluggish or overburden it with unsustainable expectations. It is possible to perform at the peak levels for short bursts, but very difficult to maintain these highest levels for extended durations. Where people are pushed too hard for too long and constantly expected to "raise the bar," it starts to negatively impact their effectiveness. When people are too busy to notice, errors emerge, critical insights are missed, and conversations are reduced.

Effectiveness by comparison is about the how well the intended purpose or expected result was accomplished. It is about the quality and sustainability of the outcome. An emergency fix to a solution may be both efficient (to prevent further losses) and effective in the short term, but may not be reliable in the long term. A more effective solution will need to replace the short-term fix in order to maintain ongoing functionality. This is where too much focus on efficiency for too long can damage effectiveness. When people start to discuss "cost effectiveness," they are really questioning the balance between efficiency (Is there a cheaper way that could work well?) and effectiveness (Will this work or will we have to do it again in the near future?). The argument between cost and quality is one that has forever been at the heart of business and project decisions and will remain so. The original light bulbs were almost indestructible. Once you had one, you rarely needed to buy another. For a light bulb company, this was not good as they needed ongoing sales. Making a product that never failed was highly effective, but was considered inefficient. Terms like "over-engineered" appeared and designers worked hard to make a cheaper light bulb that lasted 1,000 hours.[1] The actions of the Pheobus cartel in this situation planted a new seed in business mindsets that resulted in efficiency becoming more important than effectiveness, and resulted in the creation of planned obsolescence. The relationship between efficiency and effectiveness has since then been critically assessed in the development of all products and services. We emerged into the era in which competitiveness and success was judged by economic efficiency.[2]

The evolution of the mobile phone is a good example of this balance and how quality was originally perceived as effectiveness (how functional was the early phone in terms of robustness and signal connection, almost regardless of cost). However, expectations of what a phone was for dramatically changed over time. Early phone buyers wanted robust phones that lasted because phones were expensive. As phones became more reliable and the technology of phones and the infrastructure accelerated performance, they became affordable for the mass market. The phone buyer demographics and their reasons for buying a phone changed. New players with cheaper to produce, though not as robust or enduring, phones entered the market by adding features. The entry of the smartphone transformed the market. Current products are sold on coolness and app functionality rather than reliability. In fact, building in greater reliability or longer lifecycle is a cost disadvantage, because people want to buy the next new thing with better features before the hardware is likely to fail. The market evolved from a high-quality hardware product for a specific purpose into one where the product and its reliability were just a sideline in the decision about the services available. Efficiency trumped effectiveness in the new market. Players like Nokia who were slow to see this change and adapt and paid the price for that error of judgment.

Outputs AND Outcomes

Outputs (tactical, shorter-term, tangible results) and outcomes (strategic, longer-term, and more intangible aspects of decision and actions) have been discussed consistently throughout several of the earlier chapters. Again, these words are often used interchangeably and we need both for success. The key is to align them as much as possible. Any decision to act should consider the immediate impact (output) and the longer-term consequences (outcomes). Ideally, a tactical action will assist in delivery of the longer-term strategic outcome. This is not always possible, especially in an emergency. Effort sometimes needs to be expended on a solution that will not provide lasting value, but will be adequate for the short term. An example of this is sandbagging in floods. It requires a lot of energy and cost to fill and place sandbags to prevent flood waters entering properties. Then there is more work to remove all these sandbags after the danger has passed. However, the cost of placing the sandbags is less than the cost of the damage caused. A more strategic approach would be to build a bund wall on the river's edge, such that has been done in many riverside cities to reduce the risk of flooding in the first instance. This requires more effort, cost, and time, but is a better long-term preventative solution. Over the past few decades, greater attention to safety, environmental, and quality aspects of doing business are increasing the input costs. But this attention also saves lives, better protects personnel, and helps with environmental sustainability. The challenge arises if your competitors are not taking these into account and your potential clients and customers want to buy on tactical efficiency rather than strategic effectiveness. The outputs are not on an equal playing field if the outcomes are not part of the equation. Informing your stakeholders of all the interdependent characteristics of your offering or project is critical to success. You must tell how your offering or project surpasses the alternatives in terms of capability AND capacity, effectiveness AND efficiency, strategic benefit AND tactical risk mitigation, and productive outputs aligned with strategic outcomes. Although a challenge, this approach leads to strong reputation and ongoing strategic relationships.

Tactics AND Strategy

As the last few sections have highlighted, the challenge for the modern leader is how to engage your stakeholders around the outputs and outcomes you generate, while optimizing the capabilities and capacities at your disposal to ensure you use them efficiently and effectively to achieve constructive tactical results and sustainable strategic development. Without any of these, you become less competitive. This paradox of balancing seemingly opposites is the ultimate challenge for ongoing performance and reputation and explains why market leaders struggle to remain on top for prolonged periods. Most often, tactical shortcuts are taken to maintain the profits in the short term and this costs the organization in the long term. When managers are rewarded on short-term tactical results, it is difficult to get them to consider strategic aspects of the challenges they face. Tactical thinking is everywhere and impacts how we make sense of the world. The mass media post new information "to the minute" (Has the situation really changed significantly from a minute ago?—Not usually!). Stock market values are reported daily in television and in seconds in the markets themselves (Has the productivity and overall value changed significantly within these timeframes?—Not usually!). Many sales professionals are paid bonus incentives on weekly, monthly, or yearly targets (Is this going to reinforce strategic deliverables over tactical results? Not usually!).

The list of life experiences that reinforce immediate benefits of tactical reactions over proactive strategic planning is endless. The constant barrage of messages to do it now and let the future take care of itself heavily influences mindsets and negatively impacts sustainability of decisions and performance. Even some of the best organizations that featured in *Good to Great*,[3] crumbled in the 2008 stock market crash. The strategic approaches that made them great had not finally failed them. Instead, new leaders wanting faster results changed the focus to shorter-term thinking and caused their demise.

High-performing organizations proactively plan so that tactical actions form foundations of the strategic plan as much as is possible. This alignment of outputs with outcomes balances efficiency (less wasted effort) with effectiveness (ongoing benefit from the work). Software development is like this most of the time. Each minor update is about tactical fixes of existing code and a full new release is normally about strategic extensions to the functionality. If the software company is always fixing poorly coded algorithms, they have less time (capacity) to further develop the capabilities of their applications and become less competitive and less desired by customers. Get the balance between tactics and strategic actions right and the organization benefits from both responsive incremental improvements and well-timed disruptive innovations.[4] How to effectively and efficiently put this thinking into action was described in Blue Ocean Strategy.[5]

Metaphor, Symbolism, Humor, AND Political Correctness

These four topics are too big to fully include and too important to leave out. Metaphor and symbolism are deeply embedded in every language and culture. It is worth exploring how they are used and how powerful they are and embedding this in your practices. The short coverage in this section is just a small sample of how they can be used and there are entire books written on using metaphor for workplace applications For example, in broader aspects of life,[6] organizations,[7] for behavior and relationships,[8] and for understanding projects.[9] Humor can enhance performance and defuse challenging situations;[10] too little or too much political correctness can result in conflict. However, I touch on each of these slightly to include a few brief insights to whet your appetite to read more on these tricky subjects.

Language is symbolic and filled with metaphorical meanings. It has to be so that we can understand the complex concepts that we try to share with each other (or try to hide for others). Early written languages were pictograms, which represented the object in literal ways. Language slowly evolved to represent meaning in more abstract ways, though metaphorical representation and symbolic meaning remains. A huge range of research discusses the importance of symbols and metaphor and on the power of metaphor to help understand unfamiliar contexts and convey complex meaning. When we are unsure how to describe something in literal ways, we almost always use something familiar to our audience to enable them to place the new into a context they already understand: That is, a symbolic or metaphorical way to represent it. Understanding how to connect with metaphor can enable us to connect with people more effectively and communicate more productively.

Metaphor is far more common than most people realize, because they just accept it as part of their normal way of interacting. A metaphor is a figure of speech in which a term or phrase is applied to something to which it is not literally applicable in order to suggest a resemblance, for example, "A mighty fortress is our God." When something is used to represent something else, it helps people understand what you mean with greater clarity. Metaphors are in this way a symbolic connection that aids communication. Illustrative examples used to make a point include "time is money" or "argument is war." In addition to words, images and symbols can also be used as a metaphorical representation, such as the use of caricatures and metaphoric cartoons. Many of the illustrations in this book have been designed as metaphoric representations to stimulate divergent thinking and discussion about the topic and enable rich conversations. Rich pictures[11] from soft systems methodology have also been shown to be a good way to explore meaning and situations, showing the creative nature of combining imagery, story, symbolism, and language to connect aspects of ideas between people. I have been experimenting with opening conversations about various contexts using the rich pictures included in this book, which is described in more detail in Chapter 9.

Metaphor is deeply embedded into the stories, dance, and songs on which indigenous cultures around the world passed on knowledge. The military metaphor is still in wide use in business despite confrontational methods of leadership being less well accepted (though still commonly practiced). Metaphor is more easily understood when well used than jargon and other means of communication. Equally when using them, you have to be cognizant of your audience as metaphor in one culture can be quite different in another. In Western cultures, the dragon represents evil and is killed by the hero as a happy ending. In many Eastern cultures, the dragon is the hero metaphor!

Humor has a correlation with executive performance as when it is "… used skillfully, greases the management wheels. It reduces hostility, deflects criticism, relieves tension, improves morale, and helps communicate difficult messages."[12] Combining a good sense of humor with high emotional intelligence enables one to read the emotional environment to generate positive relationships and also to diffuse potential conflicts. The synergies between the two are generated when the person having them engages in sense-making and reflective practice.

It has always surprised me how little attention philosophers have paid to humor, since it is a more significant process of mind than reason. Reason can only sort out perceptions, but the humor process is involved in changing them.

—Edward de Bono

Increased awareness of political correctness in professional environments often creates a reluctance to speak up or discuss behavior. This lack of exchange of views can lead to potentially destructive interactions as people are not aware of the impacts they are having on others. Low behavioral awareness can reduce the ability to use behavior in a constructive manner to drive collaboration and reduce conflict. These dangers are magnified in the pressure cooker environment of a complex project, where the people interact closely under the added stresses of quality, cost, and scope with looming tight timeframes. Political tensions, through over- or undercorrectness, generate negative consequences. Low productivity and project failures are common, resulting in huge costs, delayed delivery of benefits, and significant stress and emotional impacts. I remember working on a large project where political interference directly caused significant delays and millions of dollars in losses. This was mainly because of poor internal relationships and overly political communication interfering with the project team's ability to get the work done. A better balance of open conversation and willingness to receive feedback early in the project may have generated some trust and enabled more straight talk to alleviate tensions and resolve matters. That project lost alignment with business stakeholders and most of the investment was wasted, when it could have generated huge benefits for the organization. Unfortunately, such stories are not unusual in politically charged business environments, or in overly politically correct organizations where no one is prepared to criticize the ideas put forward. A quick search of the Internet elicits a mass of books on the detrimental effects of political correctness. However, this does not imply that we should not be mutually respectful! We all benefit by investing the effort to achieve the "Goldilocks" sweet spot (not too much, not too little).

This chapter highlights that the words and language we use, and how we use them, have a huge impact on what we can achieve. Yet, it is rare in businesses to hear people discuss the vocabulary and preferred style of communication and interaction. Sometimes, good facilitators will explain the "rules" of engagement at the beginning of a session to try to set the atmosphere, but this is often dismissed by cynics as soft and not relevant. More active reflection on the precise words we use and why we use them helps participants to understand each other and stimulates us to reflect, before making a decision or acting. In my experience, this enhances performance and should be encouraged far more than it is.

Contributor Case Study

Paul Culmsee, Seven Sigma, Australia

Visualizing Conversations

When a global engineering company decided to bring all of their contract managers together as part of a corporate leadership retreat, they had a problem. Of the fifty key people attending from all over Australia, twenty of the most senior managers had to present the details of the contracts they managed, such as scope, how the work has changed, the challenges, wins, and any innovations that they felt need to be embedded into the rest of the organization.

The problem was the "death by PowerPoint" all of us have at some time experienced. If twenty managers presented twenty PowerPoint decks, more than a day would be spent on highly boring monologue. Few insights would be provided since the only opportunity for dialogue would be during the coffee breaks.

To address this, we conducted a series of recorded lessons-learned-type interviews over Skype with the twenty managers prior to the event. While recording interviews on video is nothing new, what was new was that we then *mapped* each interview using a tool called Glyma, which is designed to tap into the oral, experiential, and dialogue-based knowledge of teams. By mapping each interview in Glyma, we could structure each interview into logical, easily digestible artifacts by drawing out alternative ideas, questions, and lessons learned.

Once the twenty interviews were mapped, we were able to visually draw out the emergent themes and make them visible in a single, large map. Through iterating and synthesizing these themes, we were able to create a visual knowledge artifact that distilled the collective wisdom of the interviewed staff down to five core "meta-themes." All the while, we are able to link to and play from specific sections of interview video footage. By taking the workshop group through the visual map we had created, I could click on particular nodes to play back the video from the interviews, highlighting the anecdotes and stories that led to that theme being identified.

The response was that the five themes synthesized from the maps were *exactly* the areas that needed their focus, and accordingly, the rest of the day was spent utilizing collaborative sense-making approaches to identify strategic and tactical interventions to realize the opportunities and mitigate issues with each of these themes. Since we used Glyma, this artifact is interactively searchable and navigable on the corporate intranet, while still containing all of the rich stories that are never carried through to a slide deck.

Finally, we asked the participants how they felt about the process. The response was overwhelmingly positive, principally because of the time saved from putting together presentations, and the improved opportunity for dialogue when the group came together. As one of the participants aptly pointed out, "We are very good at capturing lessons, but this is the first time we learnt them."

Reflective Activities and Additional Learning Resources for the Curious Executive and Students

Applying this learning in practice

1. Make a list of words that caused confusion in your experiences and assess why this happened and what the consequences were. Share stories among your peers of how important the words used were in triggering misunderstandings and why the confusion happened.

2. Challenge how effectively you prioritize your projects. If you are a typical organization, you are likely to have a large list of approved projects that have not been fully resourced. There is probably an expectation that these will be completed within your current planning cycle, despite the specific capabilities and capacities not being carefully planned and allocated. Discuss in your groups how many times such a scenario has caused issues for your organization.

3. Discuss whether humor is used well in your organization to enhance relationships and how this is achieved. Are there examples where

damaging sarcasm is portrayed as humor that caused discomfort to some of the participants?

4. List the symbols and metaphors in your organization and share how these enhance understanding of complex situations. Use The Organizational Zoo free on-line profiler to assess the behavioral profile of your organization in different contexts. Discuss how and why your assessment differs from your peers. *www.organizationalzoo.com/profiler*

Additional learning resources:

www.intelligentanswers.com.au/KnowledgeSuccession

CHAPTER 9

Theory Informed Practice and Practice Informed Theory

Executive Summary

In this chapter, we ask why academics and practitioners don't effectively interact to generate mutual value. The opportunities for synergies are vast, but do not often eventuate because good connections between the two parties are uncommon. The key points being made in this chapter are:

- There are nuggets of gold in both sides for all parties.
- How to build stronger links and respect between theorists and practitioners?
- Why are these links important to the profession of project management?

In my 25 years working in industry I was often seen as the "academic." When I then entered a part-time academic role parallel to my consultancy practice, the academics thought of me as a "practitioner." The more this pattern became apparent, the more I realized that I had got the balance about right. Along the way I made some discoveries that I believe would help both sides be more productive, namely:

1. Academics don't read practitioner literature.
2. Practitioners don't read academic literature.
3. Lost synergy opportunities.
4. Language nuances as barriers to understanding.
5. Visualization for creative knowledge co-creation.

Academics Don't Read Practitioner Literature

Academics are taught from the beginning of their career that there is a hierarchy of literature quality. For an academic, perceived credibility declines, starting with peer-reviewed academic journals, other academic journals and academic books, followed by other books and periodicals. Even within peer-reviewed academic journals, a range of journal-ranking systems differentiate between journals based on measures of quality and impact. For example, the Australian Research Council (ARC) has a four-level ranking system of A*, A, B, and C journals. ARC[1] considers that for A* journals representing the top five percent: "Virtually all papers they publish will be of a very high quality." By comparison, a B journal (ranked in the 50 to 70 percent range) is judged as having "only a few papers of very high quality," and C journals (representing the bottom 50 percent of ranked journals) are considered as those that "do not meet the criteria of higher tiers." Academics are very actively encouraged to publish in the highest-ranking journals possible, as it impacts their career prospects and the ranking of the institution they work for. As a consequence, academics have a strong incentive to read only the journals they seek to be published in. These environmental selection pressures heavily influence the mindset of an academic to become predominantly critical. From determining what to read from where, through to the normal assessment to any written piece being a skeptical challenge of the statements made, supplemented with a detailed review of the evidence provided and the process through which that evidence was created. This is considered a healthy mindset that ensures an academic is not influenced by lower-quality literature. Such reasoning encourages a strong desire to categorically prove or disprove a hypothesis in order to make robust contributions to the knowledge in their fields. There is little tolerance for ideas that are considered half-baked, as they may contain flaws that are yet to be discovered. The process of getting something published into an A* journal is exceptionally challenging, but greatly desired. However, many academics do not achieve this highly desired outcome and suffer in this publish (well) or perish environment. Those that regularly achieve A and A* publications are revered by other academics and secure the most prestigious positions.

In such a highly competitive environment, people often do not consider literature that is viewed as contrary to their own research and reputation. If one was to try to publish a paper that was not backed by strong supporting evidence, reviewers would reject the paper or ask for it to be further refined through a long and arduous process of peer review. For this reason, literature lacking a peer review is not awarded the same level of respect and is often seen as unworthy of reading. When assessing the quality of a paper, an academic's first step is look at the number and age of references used and how the journals are ranked. Judgments about the rest of paper are made according to this initial perspective, and the paper will be returned for enhancement or simply rejected.

The term "pracademic" has emerged to describe a growing population of professionals that span the divide between academic and practitioner groups. With more postgraduate qualified professionals in the boardrooms and more universities, there is a growing acceptance of academics as advisors and of practitioners teaching. The traditional rejection of academics in industry as "boffins" (theorists who are not that practical) is diminishing to some degree. However, the race for university rankings has resulted in universities insisting that all teaching staff be PhD and teaching qualified, making it almost impossible for practitioners without a PhD to engage in teaching. The irony is there are many people with PhDs who may be great researchers, but are very ordinary, or even mediocre, teachers. Universities have lost the services of some very good teachers with great practical experience as a result of these changes. In the end, the students lose on both sides. Of course, there are good teachers with PhDs and experienced practitioners who are poor teachers, but decisions are being made purely on the qualification and not the capability of the candidates. This is an ongoing issue that will continue to cause divisions between the two sides and undermines the benefits that can be reaped from closer relationships.

This new hybrid breed of pracademics values the insights from both sides and can see the value of creating new knowledge from ideas previously lost in the gap between traditional academics and practitioners. Pracademics attempt to generate interactions that contain elements of both rigorous process and relevant outcomes to drive the creation of new knowledge and support better-informed decision making (sometimes referred to as Action Research). Case studies are the obvious example of literature that lays between academic and practical aspects of study. This is why the case study method is popular in more practically oriented education disciplines such as project management, social studies, and business. The theories, models, and tools are put to a use that has a direct result on decision making about actions to be taken. Other forms of study can be pure theory and not of use for the student in any future endeavor. Without a context to apply the theories, the content is very dry and difficult to retain, which is a significant reason to not read the literature.

Some journals, such as the *International Journal of Managing Projects in Business*, are more open to relevance-based papers that would be rejected by strictly traditional academic journals. They see this in-between market as more interested in pragmatic insights than in pure theories. By contrast, career academics are desperate to get published in A journals to maximize their career progression and promotional opportunities. However, traditional journals focus so much on robustness that the papers tend to be theoretical and weighted to heavy statistical analysis of large volumes of data. But C-suite executives want to get the message in an executive summary from someone with a proven credibility record, which is why opinion pieces in journals like *Harvard Business Review* remain popular. They offer comparatively shorter articles that make their point based on the reputation of the author, more than the volume of evidence to support the statements. This is reflective of how advice is taken in business—ask someone you know and trust and then act.

Practitioners Don't Read Academic Literature

The first challenge in traditional industry-based organizations is to get them to subscribe to more than a few academic journals. You can't read what you can't access. However, the main reason practitioners do not read academic articles is a healthy disrespect for theories and the significant cost investment. Stereotypically, they see theories and models as just ideas rather than practically implementable solutions. Theories can take a long time to mature, and by then an executive has weighed up a situation, bounced it off three trusted advisors, made a decision and either profited from it, or if reflective enough, already learned from the failure. Learning happens on the practical journey in the course of life, not in a classroom. They consider themselves too busy to read long-winded articles that pontificate about theoretical possibilities; they want 100 words on practical probabilities.

The second challenge for industry professionals is they are often seen as being nonproductive if they are sitting at a desk reading. While we all know that this is not true, there is a significant peer pressure to look busy. Reading, and talking for that matter, is not considered by many traditional business owners as productive work. Although the mindset is slowly changing, an expectation exists (sometimes self-imposed) that reading is something you should be doing on your own time. This unfortunate attitude results in many managers trying to climb the corporate ladder doing their reading at home and losing work–life balance. As modern business owners come to appreciate the importance of remaining informed with new ideas, they will start to expect the opposite; their people will balance time between learning and applying. An adoption of Pareto's 80–20 rules has found some favor with 80 percent of time spent working IN the business (spending time taking actions) and 20 percent spent ON the business (investing time to be informed and improve performance). Modern leaders want people who keep themselves informed and come with recommendations on how to implement new ideas. The source of these ideas could easily come from academia.

Lost Synergy Opportunities

Different countries and industries have quite different relationships between industry and academia. It is no accident that many of the top performers over time have fostered close relationships. Organizations such as Arup, Toyota, and GE have deeply invested relationships with academic institutions, and many such organizations have invested in their own in-house universities. The example of Arup in the boxed mini case is a shining example of how this matters for organizational performance and culture. These internal universities exist largely because the internal learnings are more practical and directly related to the organization than any learnings from an external institution. Professional development can be customized and aligned with the working experiences of the professional and immediately applied. Such action learning is optimal and far more likely to be retained and used.

What do we need to do to create the right atmosphere that connects theoretical thinkers and action-oriented practitioners? How can we create a trusted and respectful environment where synergies come from connecting the best of both worlds? Eric Weiner's book, *The Geography of Genius*,[2] explores what must happen to create remarkable work. He realized that a sense of place provided the ingredients to generate genius. The common characteristics of such places over time included:

- Availability of mentors and sponsors (to recognize and guide talent).
- Freshness (openness to new ideas for other places and encourage diversity).
- Chaos, bustle, and crossing boundaries to share ideas in a trusted environment.
- Discernment by challenging ideas to develop a constructive competitive tension.
- Genius clusters (community of practice with diversity of ideas and social conversations).
- The place itself, with the wealth to attract talent and a sense of belonging and worth.

Such an environment is difficult to create as it has seemingly opposites operating in parallel (the paradox described in other chapters): competition and collaboration, prior knowledge and fresh insights, chaos and order, critique and support. The harmony comes from harmonizing all, and this is difficult to maintain over time. Perhaps this explains why the sources of genius have changed places over time, as the intellectual and social values adjust though evolution of humanity. There is no doubt that some places have this atmosphere and are worth seeking out. Over my own career, I have traveled extensively and have always taken the time to explore some of the great places of learning, past and present, to absorb the atmosphere and try to understand what makes them tick. Weiner's book connects the dots quite nicely to build the themes you should be trying to create in your own environments.

Language Nuances as Barriers to Understanding

The language of a practitioner is very different from that of an academic. This can cause limited communications between them. Where the practitioner focuses on what may be possible and what risks are worth taking despite not knowing, the academic focuses on being certain of the process and what can be proven before acting. Ironically, a key purpose of academia is to create new knowledge and learning, yet academics hesitate to act because they are more focused on the process than the outcome. Practitioners primarily learn through taking action and especially through iterative learning cycles such as multiloop or action learning, though most of them are unaware of the theory behind why this works. Some academic researchers have a version of this in action research, which does not try to control the "experiment" but is designed to explore the context and understand in robust ways what happened. While practitioners would view this approach as sensible and pragmatic, some academic circles reject it. The mindsets and words used are very different. This can make communications effectively as different as translating across languages (such as English to Swahili). Academics have very specific words that are not commonly used in even professional English because they like to specifically highlight nuances between similar things that the average practitioner would not recognize.

This divide is exacerbated by a very different focus. Practitioners are more interested in outcomes and relevance. Academics are more interested in processes and rigor. The argument of relevance (Is what you get of use in your situation?) and rigor (Does the evidence provide a justifiable foundation for your statements?) reinforces the differences between the two groups. Each group picks at the flaws in the other's perspective, rather than leveraging the differences to learn from each other. Thus, neither group explores the other's literature because it does not deliver what they seek. Academics reject practitioner insights as too opinion-based to be credible, while practitioners reject academic writing as too theoretical to inform decisions. This is a huge limitation since both can learn enormously from each other. My own experiences have demonstrated this: When I worked in industry I was considered a "bit academic" on aspects such as risk analysis and decision making because I introduced supporting models and processes to challenge "gut feel." When I returned to academic pursuit late in my career, I would often get comments that my approaches were insufficiently rigorous and too inclusive or subjective. Although these were criticisms, I took them as compliments since hybrid approaches generate more value than those polarized at either end of the spectrum. Ultimately, all aspects—rigor, relevance, process, and outcomes—are important to good professional practice in all disciplines.

The language that academics and practitioners use and what they focus on provide insights into why academics and practitioners are like different species in diverse habitats. Table 9.1 compares the features of each to highlight why it should be no surprise that they do not understand each other. As mentioned earlier, the use of different words is almost a foreign language, which makes it difficult for them to communicate. These comparisons are obvious to most observers, but reflecting on them in one list shows the many barriers to effective communication and explains why the gaps exist. The 'isms and 'ologies refer to the academic words for

Table 9.1 Examples of stereotypical differences in focus and language of academics and practitioners

Academics	Practitioners
Robustness	Relevance
Process and method	Outputs and outcomes
Ideas	Value
Data and models	Experiences and decisions
Theories	Practice/what works
Concepts	Specific opportunities
Intellectual merit	Return on investment
Research and teaching	Apply, implement, and learning
Proof of concept	Usable practicality
Critique	Applicability
Create new knowledge	Apply knowledge to innovate
Avoidance of risk	Calculated risk-taking
Theoretical learning	Applied learning
Past-informed future development of options	Past-informed present actions
Specialized words for highly specific topics	General (often colloquial conversational) words
'isms and 'ologies	Actions and results

seemingly every field of study the practitioner thinks irrelevant. Academics need to be specific about the special terms of their field of study (that is 'ologies such as geology, physiology, or sociology) and the approaches and perspectives their research is taking to generate insights ('isms like positivism, constructivism, and connectivism). Defining terms for other academics is critical to ensuring they understand your perspective. However, if you start an interaction with a practitioner by defining, you will more often activate their snooze button. Equally, practitioners have their own jargon that people outside the field do not understand. For example, being very specific about a piece of machinery is critical to problem diagnosis in engineering. Once we understand that we all have language nuances in our own fields of experience, we can start conversations that matter to trigger new knowledge and apply it. These conversations benefit from our differences as we can bring fresh perspectives.

The list in Table 9.1 is not meant to be comprehensive. It provides sufficient examples to highlight the communication challenges between the parties. An awareness of these is the first step toward more constructive exchanges for everyone involved. As a pracademic myself with a decade of parallel initiatives in both camps, I often find myself in the role of interpreter between the industry personnel and the academics. Once expectations between the parties are clear, a facilitated conversation can be commenced around research work that generates bigger impacts, as they start to engage around each other's goals.

Parties on either side may believe that I am unfairly criticizing them, but, in reality, I am highlighting opportunities lost to lack of interaction and meaningful dialogue, not attributing blame. There are significant opportunities to bring these parties together to stimulate ideas, drive innovations, and stimulate growth once they start to see and value each other's perspectives. Connections can be made from practitioner's observations through experiences to test or extend theoretical models. Equally, theories and models can be used by practitioners to develop ideas and influence design. We start to make progress once diverse parties realize simplifying language to optimize understanding that generates superior outcomes to complicating language to suggest intellectual superiority. We can then constructively engage in critical argument to leverage differences and spark innovation.

Visualization for Creative Knowledge Co-Creation

Throughout this book, I have made an effort to include images and ideas that start conversations more than they portray "the facts." This is because a majority of people are influenced by visual stimulation. As discussed earlier, the brain in remarkably adept at filling in the gaps to interpret what it thinks is there, and sometimes sees things that are not really there. This is the fundamental strength of creative visualization to make sense of what is happening. Images can capture the essence of concepts to share them with others. Images are also useful stimulants to trigger new understanding and co-create new knowledge. The images in this book have been designed to facilitate innovative co-creation conversations to examine perspectives and interpretation across diverse audiences. Workshops to explore how differently we see things bring new ideas into the conversations, which in turn spark insights. Listening to what others see that you do not opens doors to new ideas. Following these differences to expand on your own idea, especially if done in a working out loud[3] style with others, quickly generates a breadth of ideas that no individual could have possibly provided. This gives many more ideas to work from and some completely new options to explore. Use exercise three at the end of this chapter to try this out in your own work environment.

Visualization is not a new idea. Images have been used as means of expressing human knowledge and sentiment in many ways and for many purposes. From cave paintings (for art or educating the next generation?) to maps for navigation, to illustrations in written manuscripts, visual enhancement enables a deeper understanding and clarifies the topic of conversation. Edward Tufte[4] significantly influenced the modern increase in visualization. He provided remarkable insights into how visualizations throughout history have been used to draw out the meaning buried within data. His work triggered mass interest in visual approaches to distill the essence and sense from quantitative data to inform decisions and tell stories of what happened. As computing technology and data availability increased, the data visualization industry evolved to generate mind-blowing graphics from otherwise ordinary-looking data. This included everything from simple network diagrams to "connect the dots" through to data mapping of the most sophisticated appearance.[5]

Hans Rosling[6] demonstrated just how effective visualization is by creating a short animated video from 40 years of statistics. The simple video showing the shift in the data immediately highlights the importance of the data and the messages it contains. This remarkable piece of creative visualization helped others to fully understand the changes in human demographics of the mass of data. It has engaged people who would never have cared to look at the data and has started thousands of conversations about the impacts of living in the modern world and its effects on humanity. Without the visualization, these insightful interactions would not have happened. The video has been played over ten million times and often to large audiences, so the impact is huge for sharing knowledge. A later example of the evolution of the power of data visualization through a TED video came from McCandless.[7] In the past five years, there has been a tsunami of books on the topics. This was enabled by increasing availability of Big Data sources, speed of processing large volumes of data and new algorithms to transfer raw data into insightful graphics.[8]

However, long before video was available, visualization was used to transfer understanding of complex situations and contexts. Early written language was primarily pictograms; that is, images that represented the object being discussed. The Chinese character for man is depicted as a stick image walking forward. The image for woman is similar, but with a baby on her back. Early Egyptian characters were also representative. It seems ironic that we have devolved through complex grammatical structures to abbreviations and now emoticons, which are more like early character-based languages and just as expressive. They represent the message being transferred as visualization: simple, metaphorical, and clear communication. It is equally amusing that emoticons are often added to e-mails to avoid misreading the intent of the message. The visualization sets the tone and sense for the more structured message.

Paintings, television, photographs, moving film, and video production have been used to enhance education, storytelling, and knowledge sharing, as well as simply for entertainment. In more recent times, with the advent of broadband and Internet infrastructure, the use of video for entertainment, education, training, idea sharing, and stimulating conversations has exploded. TED, YouTube, and other similar sharing sites have enabled a huge amount of understanding around a seemingly endless array of topics. My own daughter learned to knit from YouTube instructional videos and proceeded to make beanies for all her friends.

Another excellent example of the power of visualization is the RSA animate[9] (Royal Society of Arts) videos. RSA animate takes inspirational speeches, draws a cartoon-like supporting visual, and speeds it up to align with the spoken words. These drawings run as a video storyboard to support the speech soundtrack and add a great deal of depth that enhances the flow of the presenter's story. The whole picture at the end of the RSA animate speech is a summary of everything shared, making review and reflection more powerful.

Graphic facilitation[10] employs a similar style of image creation to capture the essence of conversations and workshops. The graphic artist records the conversation in a series of connected images, which generates an overall image depicting the flow of the event. These images can be shared in many ways to remind those at the event of what was discussed and to share with those not present. Many examples can be found in online image sources and on social media sites. Infographics,[11] another related accelerating field, achieves similar impacts and is increasing in popularity, especially through social media where attention spans are short, requiring graphic impact to be high.

Visualization has evolved in many possible ways to capture or highlight ideas from a range of sources. It enables people to "see" what is happening or what happened, whether this is from masses of quantitative data or from a conversation. Visualizing data together can help understand existing opportunities to shift perspectives on what is possible and also to create new possibilities in the future. It is a powerful way to express what you mean and to help you find what is meant or what could be.

Contributor Case Study

James Price, Experience Matters, Australia

Effective Management of Information Assets

Experience Matters, in conjunction with the University of South Australia, Gartner and Mike Orzen and Associates (winner of the

Shingo Prize for Operational Excellence), is conducting a research project into the barriers and benefits to organizations of effectively managing their Information Assets. Among many others, Board members and C-Level executives of organizations that include Australian Rail Track Corporation, Bell Helicopter (USA), Boeing (USA), City of Cape Town (South Africa), ConWay (USA), EDS (USA), Glacier (South Africa), Hewlett Packard (USA), Lowes (USA), National Australia Bank, Sanlam (South Africa), Verizon Communications (USA), and Wells Fargo (USA) have all participated.

We are investigating a business contradiction. Every organization studied recognizes that they have knowledge, information, and data that are of value to them, that is, their Information Assets. Experience Matters' industry knowledge indicates that the potential tangible benefits from improving the management of knowledge, information, and data are conservatively estimated at $20,000.00 per knowledge worker per year. However, despite the recognized value and the large potential benefits, every organization studied acknowledges that their Information Assets are not managed as well as they could or should be. When asked what the organization would look like if it managed its Financial Assets with the same governance and discipline that it manages its Information Asset, one Oil & Gas executive declared that the company "would be broke in a week." When invited to participate in our research, the Chair of a financial institution replied, "To be honest, I don't really know much about this area and therefore don't really think I can assist."

Stage 5 of the project is investigating the potential benefits of effective Information Management. Using a Health Check or Capability Maturity assessment, we are investigating the business impacts of existing Information Management practices, what are the potential benefits of improving those practices, and what is the contribution that Information Management makes to organizations' business performance. We are finding that the benefits are significant.

A global wine company dedicated to a program of continuous improvement has a world-class manufacturing operation, particularly its bottling plant. A winery manager decided to apply improvement principles to other parts of his organization, specifically its information and knowledge management. With only 34 staff, the winery needed a pragmatic and cost-effective solution. The organization developed: a cursory but workable enterprise architecture; a folder structure that, matching the architecture, was intuitive to staff; naming conventions for documents; and e-mail guidelines. Staff now knew what to keep, what to call it, and where to put it. Shortly thereafter, a worker in wine operations declared, "This is fantastic, we can find stuff." As the organization could recognize the financial benefit of transforming unproductive activity into productive activity, a benefits realization program was implemented. Additionally, network monitoring was set up to see exactly whose behavior had changed so that good practice could be rewarded. As much as $91,000 worth of benefit was driven by those 34 staff using their simple tools in three months, equating to a recurring benefit of $10,800 per person per year without a cent being spent on hardware and software infrastructure.

Reflective Activities and Additional Learning Resources for the Curious Executive and Students

Applying this learning in practice

1. Invest some time to join a community of practice or forum that is not aligned with your usual practices. For example, an academic could join a professional industry body and a practitioner could enroll in an academic course. This does not need to be too time-consuming or onerous. It might just be lurking in an online forum or enrolling in an MOOC (Massive Open Online Course). Persist long enough to get a feel for how they approach problems and conversations. The more foreign this feels, the longer you should stay to gain alternative views. Try to actively participate in the discussion once you have a sense of how the environment flows. Usually the best way to enter is to ask a naïve question.

2. Make a list of the words you use routinely that others in your field may not understand YOUR meaning of. It may well be a word that is in common use, but your discipline uses it differently. Alternatively, read an article that is not in your area and find words that are unfamiliar. Look them up or ask someone from that discipline what their use of the word means. This exploration can be played as a game. The person in the group who can come up with the most words others misunderstand wins. The idea is to expand your understanding of other disciplines (especially across the academic–practitioner gap), to increase your awareness of the language used, and to open up barriers to communication and stimulate the flow of ideas.

3. Select one of the images in this book and ask your peers what it means to them in the context of your organization. Each individual should reflect on their own for a few minutes and write down some ideas before a group discussion starts. This is important as once sharing starts, you each influence the other's thinking and this changes your perspective. By each one sharing what you say and why this connected with your organizations, you are co-creating a diversity of perspectives that usually leads to rich insights. A basic process that has worked many times follows:

4. Ask your participants to: Interpret what the image means to you from your own individual perspective (it may help to define a context such as learning, "our organization," and problem solving). Instruct them to write down a few thoughts before speaking with anyone else. Follow these steps:

- REFLECT on how this makes sense to you (with the defined context).
- RECORD some initial thoughts (write them as you may forget when the conversation starts).
- SHARE your insights with others at your table.
- CONVERSE about the similarities and DIVERSITY in perceptions.
- CREATE new knowledge through these exchanges.

- CONSIDER potential actions, impacts, and outcomes from these exchanges.
- ACT on these insights as soon as possible after the activity to ensure they are not lost.

Any object can be used to start these co-creation conversations. The images at the beginning of every second chapter are just examples that have been designed specifically for this purpose aligned with the context of the chapter they appear in.

Additional learning resources:
www.intelligentanswers.com.au/KnowledgeSuccession

CHAPTER 10

Leveraging Behavior as an Asset

Executive Summary

Chapter 10 explains why behavior is the most powerful force in project and other workplace environments, BOTH as a constructive and as a destructive influence. Key points of this chapter are:

- There is no such thing as no behavior, you can't "stay out of it."
- Politics are not always negative and collaboration is not always ideal.
- Knowledge creations and innovation are totally dependent on the behavioral environment that project leaders and managers create (or tolerate).

You often hear people say, "I don't play politics, I stay right out of it," which is of course a political statement in itself. Humans are social creatures and the way we interact with each other is expressed through our behavior. It is based on our values and our past (good and bad) experiences. Remarkably, most people are not as aware of their behavior as they could or should be. Behavior can be the biggest contribution to your success, and if not well expressed, the cause of your failures. Your performance will improve when you actively acknowledge that:

1. Everyone "behaves" in some form and all behavior has impact.
2. Actively planning behavior enables constructive development.
3. Behavior is a key to unlock innovation and knowledge sharing.

Everyone "Behaves" in Some Form and All Behavior Has Impact

Humans are social creatures that inherently interpret who others are through a range of signals, of which behavior is the most obvious. Other signals include who we mix with, why and where, audio signals, education level and where it was received, language, accent, body language, tone, and fashion sense. We need to recognize that we are all subconsciously judgmental! The challenge is to know just how aware you are of your own social biases and how this affects your decisions, behaviors, and actions. For most people, decisions about personal behavior are subconscious. People do not actively think about how to behave or try to control the behavioral environment around them, other than to follow social norms of the context they are in. The environment largely controls how people behave in any given situation, rather than individuals making decisions about how to interact with others. In most personal and social environments, culture, not formal rules, regulates acceptable conduct.

Culture[1] is an ever-evolving set of behavioral norms that we learn through participating in our society. In effect, culture is defined by the expected and tolerated set of behaviors a group of people desires to maintain. Our sense of identity and degree of belonging to a community is determined by how closely their set of behaviors is aligned with our own personal set. When we first interact with a new community, we are quickly assessing whether their culture is something that we identify with, and we soon get a sense of belonging or uneasiness about whether we want to remain connected. Our own culture took significant time to learn, which is based on how we interact with each other. This is passed from generation to generation through values, habits, and beliefs (often through religious influences) and openly expressed through our behaviors. It has deep and long-term foundations that are slow to change and can be quite localized.

The challenge in modern fluid formal environments, such as workplaces and project teams, is the people in the communities are changing rapidly. This makes the culture less stable and the norms harder to interpret. The culture of organizations can change quickly because of a leadership change, which can shortly be followed by a significant restructure.

As one changes the people in the community, the mix of accepted behaviors shifts, resulting in changed culture. As many organizations do not have documented rules to define the culture, culture can be challenged by different subcultures forming around strong individuals. Organizations can descend into feudalism, with factions competing for resources and displaying behaviors that would not be tolerated in more stable organizations. These situations tend to have high personnel turnover and can become quite toxic and stressful.

Some professional networks attempt to establish sets of rules to maintain an acceptable culture, usually through a professional code or a code of conduct members are expected to abide by. Many countries require an oath of allegiance to the nation and its peoples when a new citizen is inducted into their society. These explicitly stated rules define the expectations of the leadership and are designed to ensure that the new members of the society understand who they are expected to be. Very often, the laws of a community or society are based on these rules.

You can't not behave! Everything associated with how you interact with others is part of your behavior, including not interacting with others. People assess each other, both consciously and subconsciously, so you are being judged, just as you are making judgments about others. These assessments may be subconscious or, less commonly, may be deliberately structured and conscious. However, even when we try to assess others' behaviors objectively, own preferences, patterns and biases still heavily influence us. This does not mean you cannot manage and control your behavior or influence the behavior of others. It simply means that you need to be aware of what limitations and influence you provide to secure the optimal outcomes.

Too much outright rejection of others' ideas will lead to missed opportunities. Too much outright acceptance of their behavior increases the chances of disruption and conflict and reduced harmony and focus. Optimal benefits flow when you are consciously aware of your own behavior and preplan how to engage with others to secure your desired outcomes. While this does not always work, you maximize success by reflecting on your behavior and interactions, before they happen, as they happen, and after they have happened. Honestly challenging the results will enable you to engage in more productive ways in future, and discussing this with others will increase your insights. Choosing your behavior is not compromising your values. You have a range of behaviors you are most comfortable using and some you are reluctant to engage. The more you understand when to utilize each and increase the range of your behaviors, the more adaptable you become. Reflect for a moment on great leaders and you may find they are successful because they know how to say and do the right things at the right time, while also maintaining their values. This behavioral adaptability may be an innate talent or something they learned. The important point is you can enhance your behavioral astuteness and adaptability. Daniel Goleman[2] highlighted that emotional and social intelligence can be developed. Reading others' behavior and understanding your own motivating behavior are key elements of emotional intelligence. Knowing how to act on your own thoughts and how to engage with others, based on your assessment of them, are critical to this development process.

Actively Planning Behavior Enables Constructive Development

When I started my professional career as a research scientist, I thought that simply knowing the relevant facts enabled one to solve a problem. However, throughout my professional and life experiences, I have found that while facts are important, they are not the most critical factors in determining successful outcomes. In some circumstances I have been "right," but unable to effect a good outcome because I could not influence the people I was with to adopt my ideas. On other occasions, my own knowledge of the facts was incomplete and yet we achieved success because of the way the people involved collaborated and focused on the collective challenges. As these reflections grew throughout my life and career, I learned to look at situations more holistically. I began to focus on the emotional, social, and political environment as a more important determining factor. I read volumes of literature on the topic and experimented in my own situations and came to understand (as others had also done) that behavioral awareness significantly influenced one's ability to create value. It was more important than facts as there are people who have done completely unacceptable things to and with others and there are people who have amazingly productive ideas that never get supported.

What was required was an easily understood way to engage people in social conversation about behavior that was safe, built trust, and decreased conflict. Such an approach would enable people to constructively discuss the appropriate behavioral environment to address the situation at hand. Most people inherently (subconsciously) "know" how to behave in a given context (for the cultures we are familiar with) and we usually engage automatically in these behaviors. We do not behave in the same way when visiting our grandmothers as we do when attending drinks after work with professional peers. How we interact at a funeral is different from at a work function. At least I hope this is your experience, otherwise you seriously need some of the conversations we have been discussing throughout this book! The insight of value is to understand how to involve colleagues in a way that aligns their behaviors. Stimulating conscious discussion about the optimal behavior is not usually done. Being told how to behave is not something most people enjoy or appreciate. However, choosing behavior based on the subconscious assumptions of each participant is not a good option either. Facing such situations on a regular basis motivated me to create a constructive way to engage people in positive and effective conversation about behavior. This resulted in four years of research and ultimately in the creation of *The Organizational Zoo*,[3] a creative metaphor approach to understand behavioral diversity.

From the early uses of *The Organizational Zoo*, the interventions were paper-based and highly interactive. These learnings were refined to create the on-line profiler and a range of card games based on the metaphor characters that appeared in the book. This involved several approaches to gamification before this became a popular term. Participants engaged in constructively sharing their perspectives on how they should interact to align their behaviors for the best outcomes. The techniques have evolved into a range of activities and have been widely used to achieve higher performance.[4] *Organizational Zoo* activities have now been facilitated in over 14 countries and used by a wide range of organizations including NASA, the World Bank, Cadbury, the Singapore government, and educational institutions and research centers in several countries. Workshops have been successfully implemented for HR and training organizations, government departments, volunteer-based authorities, executive education services, social media and creative enterprises, insurance companies, commercial banks, food manufacturers, construction and engineering firms, and not-for-profits. This demonstrates that leveraging behavioral environments can benefit all work environments.

The ability to acknowledge that different perspectives and behaviors are assets is an important part of leadership. Recognizing each different behavior as having a place and leveraging the diversity of behavioral options provides a much more robust and resilient organization. Knowing when to sway with the prevailing winds, when to allow them to pass, and when to resist and fight against unfamiliar or unpopular currents is critical to success. It is one thing to recognize the changes and impacts, another to acknowledge what is required. To successfully implement what you believe is the best course of action is yet another skill. Managing your own behavior, and positively influencing others to follow your lead, requires a great deal of maturity and wisdom. Emotional control can generate a more conducive environment for yourself and those around you. With practice, this is possible.

Once you accept that behavior is an asset to be actively managed and you influence others to share this mindset, you are on the path to more productivity, fewer conflicts, and greater harmony. Although this may sound like a utopian hope, it is a reality for those who adopt the thinking and actions described before. While it may not be possible to create a perfect behavioral environment, you can certainly enhance the way people express their behavior toward each other, without defining and forcing a set of behavioral laws. This is achieved by creating an open environment where differences in perspectives are respected and explored, as was discussed in several of the earlier chapters of this book. Under such circumstances, behavior becomes an asset to be leveraged, instead of a source of conflict.

Behavior Is a Key to Unlock Innovation and Knowledge Sharing

Imagine working in a diverse environment where everyone was aligned and yet highly adaptable to the changing contexts. Harmonious diversity is not something that many people experience. Where it happens, people can share completely different ideas with a context and others will listen without rejection. They constructively challenge and add to the idea, rather than trying to destroy it. In this environment, we accept that seemingly opposites can coexist in productive ways to maintain a harmonious state of constant change. Constant change, itself an oxymoron, is a difficult state in which to achieve stability and to maintain a degree of control. It is like a rally driver accelerating around a bend on a dirt road and needing to steer in the opposite direction that the car is drifting to safely accelerate through the other side. Whereas most people crash the car, or do not attempt to navigate such conditions at such speeds, successful leaders keep pushing the limits of speed and acceleration while adjusting to the changing landscape through touch and feel of the wheel and the momentum. The high-performance rally driver and the inspirational leader have both developed this advanced capability through experience. They acquire a sense of what is happening in the present moment and respond in ways that enable them to adjust in the next moment.

Creating an adaptable approach to knowledge sharing and innovation is similar. The facilitator, or leader, needs to be constantly assessing the behavioral environment to ensure it is aligned with the activity at hand. They sense the momentum of the moment and the appropriateness of the interactions to adjust with provocative remarks to disrupt or insightful support to accelerate progress. This benefits from a highly refined understanding of behavior with adept skill and experience to shift the mindset of the participants. At times it is better to move them along when they appear to be stuck and other times to allow them to explore. Too much acceleration and the creativity and innovation run off the path; too little results in the ideas stagnating or participants receding into groupthink.

As the team progresses through the stages of the innovation process, balancing their behavior to align with each other and the step they are in has a strong impact on the outcomes. Once sufficient ideas are available, the open creativity needed to stimulate divergent exchanges needs to be restrained so that a few promising ideas can be developed further. This shift in the process requires a synchronized behavioral adjustment from open sharing between participants to critical analysis of the ideas. When this happens, everyone collaborates to create a range of ideas and then cull them back to the best. However, if the shift in behavior is not aligned, different participants can behave in misaligned ways that cause conflict. Once conflict starts, it can quickly become personal and emotional. The desired state is described in the section on creative friction, where the participants are aware that they are constructively challenging at that time.

Unlocking the optimal behavioral environment is a significant challenge, especially since this is undergoing constant change. However, like most worthy challenges, the more effort invested the greater the progress and return from the process. Understanding that any new way is difficult at first and acknowledging it will feel uncomfortable helps. Providing support for others to get through that early discomfort accelerates behavioral adaptability, and people soon become more comfortable working in uncertainty to generate better outcomes. Once this happens, what seemed to be rigid barriers are seen as flexible boundaries to start pushing. The irony is, every two-year-old already knows that. However, toddlers have not yet developed the behavioral maturity to manage the learning in a constructive way. As adults, we need to rediscover the curiosity of our inner child and proactively manage it with a mature understanding of behavior and social idea exchange. Now we are leading amazing creativity and innovation outcomes!

Contributor Case Study

Aaron A. Palileo, Bootleg Innovation Design, Philippines

Transforming the Operations Guy into a Brand Builder

Toward the end of 2013, a student who was part of our Master of Entrepreneurship program ventured into a new endeavor, creating his own brand of organic dog shampoo. A few months after he launched the brand, I started consulting for the organization. As someone who had spent five years in a toll-manufacturing firm that produced products for a variety of pharmaceutical and nutraceutical companies, he was still driven by ensuring his machines and manpower were at full capacity. So, everyone was a customer. During our first meetings, I realized his operations background dictated the product development process and marketing strategies in his new business endeavor. The new brand was developed without a concrete customer in mind.

I challenged him to think of a specific customer, a well-defined subsegment within the broader set of dog owners. To do this he had to immerse in various dog owner groups to really understand the values of other dog owners. He also studied the existing strategies and programs of the competitors, figuring out who their target markets were. Soon, he described his target market in terms of their motivation as dog owners.

He then had to understand that building a brand entails creating a long-term relationship with the chosen customer by satisfying their emotional needs, not only their immediate functional needs. These were customers who treated their dogs as their own children, and he needed to focus his market to this. This went against his original plans of releasing a full range of dog grooming products (i.e., soap and cologne), penetrate all pet stores in scattered regions across the country and deploy advertisements even in places that had no dog owners.

When he finally bought into this paradigm shift, the strategies started flowing easily. The new value proposition was to create a product that allowed the owner to nurture the dog; he was to "let his customers make his marketing plan." Continuing this, he did various insighting methodologies to understand his customers more and involve them in his strategizing process. He asked the customers to help him design the various product permutations—from the packaging sizes, to the scents and the features, and which kinds of events and marketing activities they were looking for.

Almost a year after the organization was launched, the brand has grown more than 3× in sales, it has penetrated at least 80 percent of its most important stores and has created a strong following from its target customers. Interestingly, one of the organization's major competitors approached him to distribute their products. Previously he instantly grabbed this opportunity; however, he declined the offer as he felt he had to focus on building his own brands.

Reflective Activities and Additional Learning Resources for the Curious Executive and Student

Applying this learning in practice

1. Invite a group from your team or community to discuss how they feel about the behavioral environment you engage in. Before beginning this conversation you should agree that the interaction will be open and honest with a view to constructively understand each other's perspectives. It should be focused on the behaviors and not name individuals. If at any time you (as the leader or facilitator of the conversation) sense that the interaction is becoming political or personally targeting individuals, you should state this and either moderate the behaviors or stop the conversation. A good conversation about behavior will evoke curiosity and be a little uncomfortable, but it should never get to the point where people feel threatened, persecuted, or excluded. This can be a significant challenge in a mixed group, but is worth persisting with while participants buy into the idea that the outcome is to make it a positive learning experience for all involved. *The Organizational Zoo* profiler or character cards can assist this dialogue.

2. Gather a group together to discuss how adaptable your team or organization is. Think of a range of situations in which your team was successful and was not. Compare how the team reacted when successful versus when it failed. Was the level of reflection the same? How deeply were the reasons for success or failure discussed and how effectively did the team learn from each other's perspectives of this? If the group is a mix across several organizations, briefly share a story from one organization to set the context and then allow others to ask questions about it to drive the conversation and solicit learnings. Almost invariably, when this is done as a constructive interaction, one story quickly leads to another from another organization. Try to dwell long enough on one to optimize the benefits and insights before moving on to the next.

3. Think about how creative and innovative your organization is (remembering that they are quite different processes). Some organizations

are very creative but struggle to harvest the ideas through their innovation process to create value. Others can be quite innovative when the ideas come, but are not that great at the ideation process. This is often because the two processes require different thinking and behavior. A common approach is to have a creativity team and an innovation team. However, then the ideas do not necessarily flow that well between them. How much more effective could your organization be if the idea to valued product or service interactions were completely aligned in knowledge flow and behavior? What specific actions would enable your organization to achieve this?

Additional learning resources:
www.intelligentanswers.com.au/KnowledgeSuccession

CHAPTER 11

Being a KNOWledge SUCCESSion Leader

Executive Summary

Chapter 11 brings all the earlier aspects of projects together in a way that enables the reader to see how they can be integrated with and adapted to an emergent and complex environment. Understanding context and being confident in uncertainty are critical to doing this well. Key points of this chapter are:

- Leadership of projects is complex and can't be optimized by simplifying everything.
- The Iron Triangle is just a foundation for effective project leadership, not the entire story.
- We must reflect on what success is and why it varies with stakeholders and over time.

We explored in Chapter 1 how the world is becoming projectized and the impacts of this. Our path though the previous chapters has considered insights into why, who, what, how, when, and where we can co-create value and for whom we achieve this. We now decide how we optimize this. Uncertainty can be viewed as a source of anxiety or as an opportunity: It just depends on your perspective and level of aversion to risk. Whatever perspective you choose, sustained achievement is likely to involve combining many of these principles of KNOWledge SUCCES-Sion through implementing projects.

In doing so, we can benefit from:

1. Leading project teams to optimize outcomes.
2. Thinking, feeling, and acting beyond the Iron Triangle.
3. Knowing the elements of success.

4. Doing more of the things that generate success.
5. Becoming and being successful in ways that amplify sustainable mutual benefits.

To a large extent, this chapter is a connecting summary of the concepts covered in greater length in other chapters. Although this summary might seem better at the end, it is only once you combine these insights in creative ways that you effectively engage your stakeholders. So the impacts described in Chapter 12 happen as a result of being a KNOWl-edge SUCCESSion Leader, which in turn is an outcome of mastering and connecting the concepts from Chapters 1 to 10. This chapter highlights the bridges between the topics to connect them, as the specific details of each topic are covered in earlier chapters. This chapter accelerates your success by enabling you to connect the diverse range of concepts through a leader's lens.

Leading Project Teams to Optimize Outcomes

Traditionally, professional project education and training is focused on management and skills. As a result, project professionals have finely developed skills and capabilities built around the implementation of projects and processes with an emphasis on control and keeping it the same. That is, vigorously managing scope, process, and tasks through a predetermined plan. Project managers are taught to control activities by the defining characteristics of the Iron Triangle (generically: time, quality, resources and scope, though this varies depending on the source) to the point where changes are seen as risks to performance. As such, preventing scope creep is a closely guarded aspect of project management.

This is understandable if one assumes that no new knowledge will be created during the implementation of the project, which is rarely true. The positivist attitude that everything can be controlled to isolate an initiative or experiment so that all goes according to the predefined plan is sadly lacking in reality. Initiatives managed in this way are limited to the original expectations and cannot benefit from unexpected opportunities that emerge and are not as adaptable to unpredicted risks. This results in underperformance compared with what they could have achieved (as opposed to delivering exactly what was expected). The outcomes achieved are heavily influenced by the mindset adopted. In her insightful book, Carol Dweck[1] proposed that there are two clear types of mindset, fixed and growth. A fixed mindset assumes that achievements are largely determined and our abilities cannot change much; so what is the point of investing effort and trying harder. However, a growth mindset believes that we can all enhance our performance by investing the time, effort, and resources to improve. Given you are reading this book, you likely have a growth mindset, as you are seeking new ideas on how to improve. Those with a fixed mindset are too busy to read this book and are toiling within their comfortable, known patterns of behavior.

There is little doubt that successful leaders have a growth mindset and that this is a key aspect of their success. They are able to see future possibilities that do not exist yet and adapt their knowledge, skills, and behavior to make them happen and bring the benefits to reality. These leaders stimulate their ability to learn faster and remain at the leading edge with a firm belief that continuous development (professional and personal) is an enjoyable lifetime pursuit. They subscribe to the principles described by John Medina in *Brain Rules*[2] that human brains have evolved to learn rapidly. By nurturing an optimal environment and the right habits, we can accelerate our learning and performance. Paying conscious attention to aspects of our lives such as exercise, sleep, stress, and sensory stimulants enables us to get a better balance and enhances our performance. Neuroscience and medical studies since late last century have firmly debunked the old thinking that the brain does not develop significantly in adults. A plethora of literature around neuroplasticity and ongoing brain development was triggered by Norman Doidge's book, *The Brain That Changes Itself*.[3] We now know that anyone can enhance their brain performance, providing they have a growth mindset. If you believe you cannot achieve this, you may have created a self-limiting and self-fulfilling prophesy. To be an effective project leader you benefit from proactively adopting these principles. Continuously develop your mindset to constantly evolve the way you see and interpret the world. Constantly challenge yourself to perceive what is possible, rather than what is known. A manager focuses on problems and risks in the present, based on past knowledge and patterns. A leader creates new patterns of thinking and behavior by engaging their followers in co-creation of concepts to resolve unknown problems in uncertainty. In doing so, they generate capabilities and new opportunities for all involved. This is achieved by taking calculated risks and reflecting deeply on both successes (maybe they could have been even better) and failures (was it the assumptions, ideas, or the processes that caused us to get it wrong and how can we act differently next time).

As leaders, we are role models to others. They will imitate what we do rather than what we say but do not do ourselves. You become a leader by demonstrating you are a good role model through your actions. You cannot talk of things you will do to motivate followers without doing them (at least not for long, as many politicians have discovered).

A leader is best when people barely know he exists, when his work is done, his aim fulfilled, they will say: we did it ourselves.

—Lao Tzu

Thinking, Feeling, and Acting Beyond the Iron Triangle

While the elements of the traditional Iron Triangle (shown at the center of Figure 1.3) are important to project management, they have little influence on project leadership. Time quality, cost, and scope are all important aspects to manage to ensure projects are delivered efficiently and effectively. However, Excellent, But Not Enough (EBNE) the term coined by Edward de Bono, applies to them. While these elements are tangible and tactical input aspects that define the project, they do not engage team members to passionately pursue the project outputs and outcomes. Successful leaders engage their teams by highlighting the meaning and value created beyond the project itself. It is beyond the successful project that value is created and the legacy, credibility, and reputations of those involved remembered. The challenge for project management education is to focus beyond the tactical, inner task components of projects and become more inclusive of the outer, more strategic and human factors.

Good project leaders understand that attention to the intangible aspects generates significant benefits to the inner components. For longer-term success of any initiative, the stakeholders need to be led toward a common goal and engaged to participate so that ownership can be transferred and the outputs effectively adopted into new practices. The project leader who engages stakeholders throughout the project achieves a more effective handover to the owners at the end. This benefits from a sophisticated set of soft skills and realizes greater ongoing intangible outcomes beyond the project. Attention to aspects such as cultural and behavioral changes needs to be effectively communicated, understood, and developed to maximize the value of the project. Too often a project delivered on time and on budget becomes totally wasted because stakeholders are not effectively prepared to take ownership of the initiative. Often they do not understand the value in them doing so. The inner triangle is about delivery of tasks and measuring completion (what, when, how, and who does), while the outer triangle is about leading the emotional, social, and cultural changes. These changes generate the long-term value creation and ultimately determine success from the investment in the project (why and who benefits).

Investing leadership capabilities beyond Iron Triangle aligns the future development cycles of the organization as a whole. This more strategic approach creates synergies across portfolios or projects and prioritizes the right projects. That is, projects aligned with each other and the desired direction of the organization. Project portfolio prioritization with business vision and goals is one of the most poorly performed activities in many organizations, resulting in poor allocation of resources and wastage. This happens because of disconnection between strategy development and implementation owing to poor communication of purpose and intent. The disconnect can be overcome through stronger relationships and better targeted two-way communications using language familiar to the receiver of the information rather than one-way broadcasts in the language of the transmitter. Such communications keep stakeholders engaged and reinforce the bigger picture aspects of why the projects are undertaken, how they are communicated, and what was learned from them.

Knowing the Elements of Success

I considered for some time what the elements of success are and was challenged to define this for myself, let alone anyone else. As we discussed earlier in the book, success is such a subjective factor. However, I think there are some common factors. A useful activity to help people define success for themselves is to engage in conversations with others on the essential elements of success and their relative importance. Of course, there will be different opinions, but this is exactly what you want people to understand. In an activity like this with postgraduate students in business and project management, I use 60 elements from this book as conversation starters and ask students to summarize in a creative way, providing the word cloud in Figure 11.1 as an example. This creative activity can develop a rich and meaningful understanding across project team members about the most important elements for them as a team and can help the team prioritize and align their thinking and actions. It is a good idea to encourage them to exclude some words and phrases from the list or add new ones. After all, it is their success they are discussing, not exclusively yours. A leader is successful more through how they engage others to perform than on their own individual contributions.

It is better to lead from behind and to put others in front, especially when you celebrate victory when nice things occur. You take the front line when there is danger. Then people will appreciate your leadership.

—Nelson Mandela

Figure 11.1 One creative expression of elements of success, among many possibilities

Doing More of the Things That Generate Success

Earlier in this book we explored Knowing (knowledge), Doing (skills), and Being (behaviors and attitudes) as the primary aspects of capability. We all know someone who is brilliant, but hard to get along with. Equally, we all love someone who has significant knowledge and skill limitations. Being a successful leader is about understanding imperfections and having a constructive mindset about them. Successful leaders know their own capabilities and the limitations. Smart leaders surround themselves with other smart people who have complementary capabilities, so together they are more powerful by balancing each other's strengths and weaknesses. You are as powerful as your trusted and engaged network.

Figure 11.1 explores one perspective of the elements of success, which is the first stage in understanding success. Without knowing what success is, it is hard to achieve. The subjective and personal nature of what you consider to be success makes it an excellent topic of conversation to explore with others. For some it may be based on fame or financial independence. For others it may be as simple as happiness and personal sense of worth. However, in a project or business environment, exchanges of perspective on success are important to engage around so that we are clear on what we are collectively trying to achieve. It is possible that success for one person is very different from another and perhaps almost the opposite. Without such conversations it is difficult to achieve alignment, and with such conversations it is easier to see the challenges we face and the diversity of views that we need to consider for everyone to celebrate with equal enthusiasm.

Think about success as an outcome of what you do rather than an object to seek. Leading others toward success is usually more about co-creating an understanding of success than defining what it is. One good example experienced in my career was a leader who simply asked, "What will good look like?" This question inspired significant conversation about various elements of value that our major project would create for a range of beneficiaries and why these were important. The discussions were both motivational and informative. If the person involved had called us together to tell us his idea of what we needed to do and why from his own perspective only, it could have had the opposite impact.

All projects and environments are different. Leaders and their followers benefit from taking an emergent approach and exploring what works for them and what is not working. Reading the mood and nature of the team interactions is critical to success. Observing what works in a sustainable way and doing more of it, while diminishing those things that are not working well or adjusting your approach to them is a good way forward. Of course, your approach will be informed by your past successes and failures, but do not allow these to dominate your current and future approaches. As you go into future situations, contexts, cultures, and stakeholder expectations are different and this usually requires a degree of adaptation of your "proven approaches" to optimize what you can achieve with new challenges and opportunities.

Being Successful in Ways That Amplify Sustainable Mutual Benefits

Ultimately, most people remain in relationships that generate mutual value exchange and leave those that are a one-sided flow of giving without reciprocal value. The traditional Chinese principle of *guanxi*[4] applies to all cultures if relationships are to be sustained. Although some argue that *guanxi* is akin to corruption (because business transactions are effectively kept within the known network rather than allow free access for all, to all opportunities), there is little doubt that trusted networks are the basis of sustainable and strategic partnerships. Most people would rather maintain and build stronger partnerships with those they know and trust and who have a proven history than simply throw each partnering relationship to the lowest bidder each time they plan a strategic development.

This is an excellent example of how differently people perceive "right and wrong" and what is valued. Eastern cultures value longer-term strategic partnerships built on prior joint experiences and trust and provide preferential treatment to maintain those relationships. In some Western countries, this type of thinking is considered to be corruption and is to be avoided to enable free trade. Many Western government systems have laws preventing preferential treatment. A similar dichotomy of mindsets can be seen with respect to employment. In Asian cultures, there is a strong preference to employ someone known to the family or network, on the basis that an insider will have greater loyalty and trustworthiness. In the West, this is considered nepotism and there are usually tight restrictions on what should happen to keep decisions focused on the most credentialed person for the role. The key point is that what is valued in different relationships varies in different cultures and organizations. This is a significant consideration when leading mixed culture international teams (and often the cause of some conflict and misunderstandings).

The concept that people subconsciously have ingroups (those considered part of our network) and outgroups (those who are not) is well highlighted by psychologist and behavioral scientist Richard Crisp in *The Social Brain.*[5] He explained how our inherent biases influence our decisions and how, as we have evolved, some people have adapted away from competitive thinking to see more benefits flowing from collaborative thinking. This shift in mindset requires us to rewire our neural networks to see mutual benefits in different ways. His argument is that leveraging diversity encourages creativity, innovation, and growth; he even states this is essential to our survival as a species. As we shift our mindsets to become more collaborative, we change cultures and how we interact, thereby evolving human society. A leader who can understand this potential and convince their followers that there is greater mutual value in collaborating than competing can achieve more and harness their followers' total energies.

This may be easily said, but can be extremely difficult to achieve, for all the reasons highlighted. Sometimes, an individual is not sure of their life and professional priorities. So, to understand what everyone in your project or circle of influence wants and then provide that to each individual requires a remarkable amount of insight, emotional intelligence, and energy. This is why influence is a key characteristic of leaders. It is easier to bring people toward your own vision by inclusive interactions than try to understand everyone at the individual level.

Being a KNOWledge SUCCESSion leader involves stepping up to mentor and coach the next generation of leaders to be better than we were able to be. It requires supporting them to make the sustainable decisions that we did not always make and being open to their new ideas as well as sharing past wisdoms. They are going to need all the help we can provide and may not always want to be restricted by our "past knowledge."

However, engaging them in *Conversations That Matter* around these complex challenges will certainly accelerate mutual benefits for those involved and beyond.

Contributor Case Study

Stuart French, Delta Knowledge, Australia

Continuous Improvement Is a Time-Proven Strategy

Several years ago, a medium-sized, high-growth company was undertaking a large system implementation project, consolidating five legacy systems into one central ERP solution.

This was seen as a way not just to reduce rework and improve data quality, but also to:

1. Discover and share best practice.
2. Consolidate local anomalies.
3. Piggyback positive change efforts on the back of the ERP project.

The rapid growth of the company had resulted in a multisite workforce with custom procedures at each site, tailored solutions for large customers, and different legislation in each state. On top of this, due to the rapidly evolving entity structure, there were complex intercompany transactions and no national operational leadership, leading to the rise of site managers responsible for every part of their local business units.

This had led to a schism in the way the business was seen. To the executives, SOP meant STANDARD Operating Procedures. To the local staff, SOP stood for SPECIAL Operating Procedures. We needed a way to reconcile these both vertically and horizontally across the organization chart.

Finding a Solution

We needed to understand current operational routines and exceptions before kicking off the larger project. The business required a tool that would allow secure remote access to record current practice and then encourage conversation and debate. This second part was critical. The complex processes had built up over time in response to customer needs in an increasingly tight budgetary environment. As such, no single person in the company could clearly define the problems, and yet everybody had their own ideas for solutions.

The local processes and procedures had the advantage of direct local knowledge behind their creation, but at the same time had not been validated for efficiency either at the technical or at national levels.

The project team selected a cloud-based Wiki costing just $15 a month. It was easy to use, allowed commenting or direct editing, and a hyperlink function to join related issues/procedures. Over a six-week period, each state entered a page for each procedure based on templates provided. They were then encouraged to read the procedures from other factories and discuss if they were different from their own. To our surprise, this part of the process resulted in an evolution of the procedures as new ideas, possible pitfalls, and novel solutions were discussed. An equal emphasis was placed on recording "Why" we do things besides "What" they actually do and staff were allowed to use the phone for this too, as long as they recorded the results in the Wiki.

Far from being just a collection method, co-creating a procedure Wiki created common understanding across the business, made the end users feel like they had a voice in the project and assisted greatly with user adoption during the training and Go Live phases of the project.

Putting It to Work

The project team used the resulting knowledge base in a variety of ways.

After a review and analysis, they facilitated discussions on key areas of possible conflict. Local managers were involved so they got a better understanding. In some cases executive members were included so they could see why the business was more complex than they realized before we asked them for strategic direction.

With a focus on the minimization of costly customizations to the upcoming ERP, conflicts between state differences were resolved as much as possible. Some hard decisions had to be made, but with everything being explicit, management could better see what the impact of their decisions would be.

The knowledge base was then used as the starting point for the vendor-run implementation workshops and finally to build before/after training scenarios to assist with change management of common tasks. The process ran smoothly with just one extra pilot workshop being required beyond budget and that was for an area that had not been included in the initial scope.

Moving Forward

Once the project was complete, the Wiki was downloaded as an HTML file and the online platform shut down. Now, six years later, many of those experienced staff have left and been replaced; however, the file is still occasionally referred to as a snapshot of best practice before the consolidation.

Reflective Activities and Additional Learning Resources for the Curious Executive and Student

Applying this learning in practice

1. Invite members of your team to develop a different mindset on a particular challenge you are experiencing. This is not an easy thing to achieve because current thinking often blocks out-of-the-box ideas. You may need to do something creative first to open the minds of the team and shift the context in which you are able to envisage the challenge. Changing the language such as problem to opportunity can help. Drawing the challenge as a metaphorical image or cartoon (as described earlier in this book) may also work. Telling an out-of-context story (such as a fairy tale or fable) can lead to creative conversations that generate good outcomes. The initial aim is to experience

mindset change rather than to create a solution. Once the mindset change has been achieved, many of the self-limiting barriers lift and a number of solutions will usually flow.

2. Explore what your team considers success to be. Ask, what does "good" look like? Or propose another similar provocative question. Generate a list of words and phrases and prioritize them as a team explaining why you believe they should be in this order. Associate the words with specific desired outcomes from the project and also with personal desired impacts (e.g., ongoing employment, reputation, credibility, and financial reward). Reverse brainstorming is an alternative approach to this. It asks the ridiculous or opposite question, such as how can we destroy team spirit (or similar)? This usually provides a tsunami of responses, which can then be collated as a good foundation list of what NOT to do.

3. Think about how you can pass on your own personal insights to others to assist them in quickly developing your level of understanding. Consider how mutually beneficial a peer mentoring arrangement could be either in groups or as one-to-one informal relationships. We all have a vast amount of valuable experience that can benefit others, as others have for us. The benefits only flow if we open the paths through which the value exchange can be facilitated so that all parties receive value. Experiment with one-to-one and small-group peer mentoring in projects in both informal and formal ways to see what works for your team relationships.

Additional learning resources:
www.intelligentanswers.com.au/KnowledgeSuccession

CHAPTER 12

Influencing Stakeholders to "Buy In"

Executive Summary

Chapter 12 reinforces the need to constructively influence all affected parties, not just the key people and team members. Key points of this chapter are:

- Being a credible and trusted role model by enabling knowledge application and stimulating learning for all parties.
- Leading sustained success and creating willing followers through establishing identity and belonging and respecting and leveraging diversity.
- Developing trusted and strategic relationships beyond the immediate project.

It is one thing to be successful in your own right in your own world, but it is another thing to influence others to join you to amplify this success. Sharing your knowledge, skills, capabilities, and ideas to motivate others to create value is the ultimate measure of high-performance leadership. Real leaders achieve this through:

1. Inspiring willing, intelligent followers;
2. Sharing success and kudos;
3. Rewarding participation fairly;
4. Stimulating diversity, identity, and belonging; and
5. Creating a safe-fail environment to build trust.

Inspiring Willing, Intelligent Followers

The world is full of great ideas that never succeed. That is, their potential never emerged to generate value. One of the key reasons is that the idea did not influence enough potential "buyers" or followers to embrace the product or service. This is not just about marketing: It has wider implications. A good idea needs to be nurtured, refined, developed, and eventually launched in a way that excites and engages your target stakeholders and reduces or mitigates negative impressions and impact on others. Trust and reputation are essential components of the engagement equation. You must lead others to connect with your idea from pitch, to delivery and ongoing value creation. Success is determined by how well you can create an initial impression and then follow through with uncompromised customer support and ongoing innovation.

To lead people to engage with you and your ideas, products, projects, and services requires you to create and maintain willing, intelligent followers. Temporary, nonthinking followers are not only easily attracted, but also easily distracted. The attention span of nonthinking followers is short and disloyal. For sustained success, all three of these words are critical: *willing, intelligent*, and *followers*. *Willing* because you want people to want to follow what you advise. They have a desire to adopt your offering as their own and be proud to tell others they like your brand and why. *Intelligent* because you want them to have thought about their relationship with you and your offering and made a conscious decision to support your idea, project, and brand over others. You want to evoke both an emotional and a rational connection between your customer and your offering (project, concept, idea, service, enhancement, etc). An emotional connection usually forms more quickly than a logical one, but can be more fickle. A rational connection, while slower, can be more sustainable in the longer term. This combination of heart and head stimulates greater loyalty over time. Ongoing support and innovation strengthens the relationship in longer term and builds credibility and trust.

This trio of factors (emotion, credibility, and logic) has been known to be the foundation of persuasion for millennia. Aristotle wrote about the importance of combining Ethos (credibility, trust, and reputation), Pathos (emotion, metaphor, and relationship), and Logos (rationale, facts, data) in *On Rhetoric*.[1] Marketers have used this basic approach to persuade people to buy products and services ever since. Unfortunately, project managers do not usually get training in pitching ideas or communicating to mixed audiences and thus often do not get their ideas adopted and supported.

Communication that influences others benefits from combining the relevant aspects of the situation without overcomplicating the message. Leaders who simplify their communication about complex concepts to include all stakeholders have greater chances of being followed. This is not as simple as it sounds and requires a strong grasp of all the concepts covered in this entire book. Oversimplification will not provide sufficient understanding to enable effective completion of the task and may not engage the target audience. Over complication will confuse the audience and disengage them. Experience and knowledge of your audience both significantly impact your effectiveness as a communicator. The ability to read the audience and see who is following you helps customize the message for each member of your audience. Where possible, it is helpful to break up your audience into individuals or groups with similar perspective and background so that you can engage them with a common language. By this I mean the language of finance, or quality, or other type of jargon.

So the key question is how do you lead and communicate in order to create willing, intelligent followers?

Sharing Success and Kudos

The first step to inspire others is to lead by example through generating success and sharing the benefits and kudos. People are attracted to success and enjoy being considered part of the kudos it generates. This applies to all aspects of human life, from sporting endeavor, to political parties to intimate relationships, to organizations, and project teams. People engage with and follow those they see as role models. People want to be like their role models and to be associated with what they do. Followers respect their role models. Followers see themselves as part of a common identity with leaders and wish to achieve similar feats in future. Humans are incredibly influenced by strong role models, but are diverse in what they believe success to be. For some, simple fame (or even notoriety) engages them to follow. For others it is wisdom, physical talent, or demonstrated capability. NASA and Cirque du Soleil (see mini case studies) provide great examples of commercial and creative achievement through sustained success. What they have done is vastly different, but both excite their stakeholders with their achievements. Although most people outside of these organizations know they cannot be part of them, they have a strong connection triggered by a deep respect and curiosity for their accomplishments. Cirque du Soleil shows tour the world to packed audiences for 15 years after they were created; some places like Las Vegas have permanent performances. Compared to most other entertainment organizations, this is remarkable longevity. NASA has one of the most popular websites in the world, with people of all ages and cultures proactively engaging with them. NASA research has generated a vast number of commercial spinoff industries (from battery technology to communication to food preservation and design to list a few) that have changed the way the global human population interacts.

Such success attracts attention and a sense of identification with the brand. This does not happen by accident. Success (and potential future success in the case of projects) is amplified by well-crafted and targeted communication. In a prior publication I described the "Five C Cycle."[2] This cycle shown in Figure 12.1 that every project or initiative begins and ends with communication and communication is the fuel throughout.

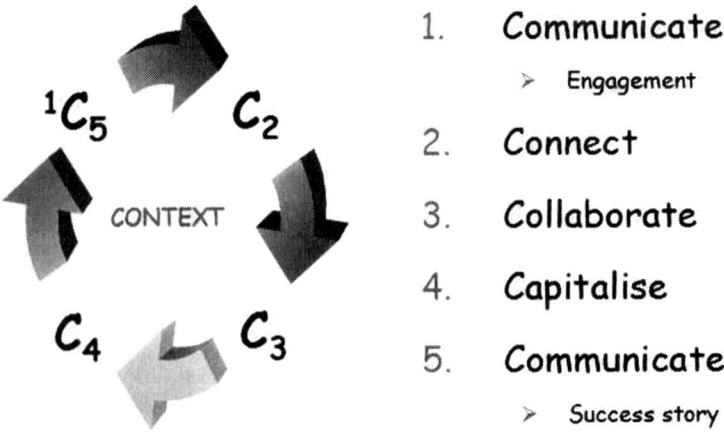

Figure 12.1 The Five C Cycle for sustained success

The Five C Cycle starts with communication (C1) to engage people around the ideas we want them to engage with. If we do this well, they will connect with us and the idea and become part of the initiative it creates. The connection (C2) leads our growing body of followers to collaborate (C3) to build and deliver the initiative, resulting in participants generating benefits for stakeholders (C4, Capitalize). Having created value, we now amplify our success by sharing these stories with others to increase followership and share the scope of the benefits. Sometimes, plans do not get delivered as expected and a project, initiative, product, or service does not perform to expectations. In such cases, benefit can still be gained through a reflective analysis to determine lessons learned. In such cases, C5 communicates the learning points and how a similar challenge may be approached in a different time or context. This approach has been applied and shown to be beneficial over a long period of time.

A common error, especially among technically trained professions such as technical, scientific, and financial fields, is to just transmit the facts; that is, to share the factual aspect of the initiative, or worse simply order people to do what is "obvious and logical." While this may be the appropriate action such professionals learn from their experience, it is deficient in two ways. First, humans are social beings whose decisions are heavily influenced by emotion. The emotive response has been processed in the subconscious brain before the rational considerations are processed. This results in the rational assessment being biased by the faster emotional reaction. It is hard for people to override their feelings about the offering. Thus, if people feel good about the offering, they will find rationale to support the logical aspects. However, if people feel challenged by the concept you are sharing with them, they will subconsciously find excuses to disengage. It is important to find emotional connections between your audience and your ideas.

A simple way to engage people around a concept is to craft a pitch that takes the target audience through a process showing them the connections so they grow to like the idea. Figure 12.2 explains how to do this to gradually bring them toward your desired level of support.

The best approach is to address the message specifically to a challenge or an opportunity dear to your stakeholder. This can often start with a leading question or statement ("you know how we are always having trouble

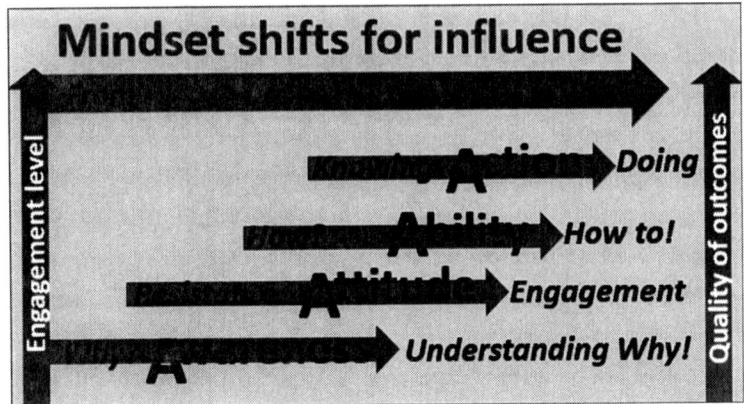

Figure 12.2 Stakeholder pitch to optimize positive influence

with …"). It can be a positive or negative statement, to get attention, but needs to become positive quickly to ensure you keep the stakeholder's attention. Once you have connected the stakeholder to your project by leveraging their emotional tags (the points they care about), you have their attention. Attention is the foundation of building attitude. Now you show that you have a potential opportunity to create value around the challenge or opportunity, which interests them in doing something about it. It generates the support you require from them to act, but not yet the capability to do so. From this attitude of intent to act, we can strengthen our case by showing what abilities we need to generate the desired outcomes. This may be highlighting capabilities, knowledge, specific people, or other resources required to achieve success. If you show you have the risks covered by explaining the concerns about the ability to achieve success, the stakeholder can then see a path forward and is more likely to act.

This sequence of creating *Awareness* to build *Attitude* to highlight *Ability* to generate *Action* is critical. Approaching this sequence the other way round most often generates rejection, because people become emotionally disengaged unless there is a strong hierarchy or a crisis. Demanding *action* of stakeholders without demonstrating an *ability* to deliver creates an *attitude* of resistance and dissent, because they have no *awareness* of why the *action* needs to be taken or the benefits of taking it. This process could involve a three-minute pitch for something simple or may take multiple interactions over a longer period for complex change projects.

A second common error leading to early project rejection is to only involve those supportive of your cause. While enthusiasts and supporters are needed, they only present one side of the argument. They will pro-actively follow your lead and address actions required to achieve success. However, for most projects and initiatives, there are other stakeholders who do not support your initiative. They too need to be engaged to opti-mize success, even if just to mitigate the negative impacts they may have. We discussed stakeholder categories in Chapter 5 as Sponsors and Allies (high influence and support), Enthusiasts (low influence, high support), Opponents or Adversaries (high influence, low support, or aggressively against), and Watchers (low influence and support).

Without making an effort to understand who in your team, orga-nization, and beyond fits each of these categories and why, you are in danger of disengaging your stakeholders. Stakeholder analysis is import-ant as it ensures you are communicating with each stakeholder (or group of stakeholders) in a way that reflects their impact on the proj-ect (positive or negative). The positive energy and support of sponsors and enthusiasts can be used to increase awareness and provide tangible resources and influence others. The political challenges that adversar-ies present need to be carefully managed to mitigate against any detri-mental impacts. Business is a strategic and competitive endeavor that requires balance between value-creating and value-destroying activities. Sometimes, adversaries are not immediately obvious: Your adversary is not necessarily a stereotypical political enemy who hates you and your project. It could simply be another respected peer who is competing for resources and funds and the organization can only support your ini-tiative or theirs. Often, both initiatives are worthy, but both cannot be prioritized at that point in time. Although not-for-profits and charities are theoretically outside the realm of competition, the reality is they too experience competition for resources and attention both internally and externally. Being aware of such challenges is essential to success (and sometimes even to moving beyond initiation). In my experience, many business leaders and project managers only pay lip service to stake-holder analysis, at their own peril. Done well, a robust and prolonged stakeholder engagement and communication plan is a huge asset to any initiative.

Rewarding Participation Fairly

Another way to convert stakeholders to willing, intelligent followers is to ensure fairness in the eyes of the stakeholders. Organization decisions are often made in imbalanced ways and are biased by the experiential limitations and knowledge of those making them. In fast-paced, highly siloed, and specialized organizations, people make rushed decisions on the resources and knowledge immediately available to them. While this is efficient and understandable in the short term, collections of quick-fix decisions over time negatively impact longer-term outcomes. If decision makers were aware of the wider implications of the decision, they might decide differently, but you cannot know everything. This is why engaging through communities of practice and social groups of trusted colleagues is essential to productivity. Participating in diverse conversations provides some immunity against blinkered and rushed groupthink. It enables us to find and ask challenging questions to elicit other relevant aspects of the decisions we take. This investment up front can pay huge dividends later. Every successful entrepreneur knows that failures are just a part of success. However, they also know that failures need to be swift and early in any initiative, before they become too costly. Success is a fine balance; this is more effective when we invest in divergent thinking early in the initiative. Participation is too often seen as time wasting, and it can become so if political procrastination is rife. However, well-facilitated participation with the right people has been an invaluable generator of productivity throughout human history[3] and should be encouraged.

The value of participation is often underestimated by others who are not aware of the benefits it brings to the participant. Mentoring relationships can be a good way to guide how effective participation is as they provide an alternative perspective to challenge the benefits. Self-reflection is powerful, and reflections with others in trusted environments accelerate the benefits and power of this process. This can be beneficial from both sides by engaging people to participate more in beneficial activities and by extracting them from participation in activities that do not add value to them and others.

I personally participate in a number of communities in various ways and at different levels. In some I am part of the leadership. While in others I am more of a follower and learner. Some are face-to-face regular gatherings and others are completely virtual. I am a regular contributor in conversations in some and more of a lurker in others. They each bring different benefits in different ways and some I contribute to more than others. Providing a considered perspective for others to reflect on (rather than telling them they are wrong and you are right) is a key part of being a role model. Having a voice and being prepared to constructively disagree helps others to see things differently. Admitting when you are wrong is also a part of this.

Stimulating Diversity, Identity, and Belonging

Understanding the power of including others in discussions and decision making is another step toward creating willing, intelligent followers. This includes demonstrating what it means to "belong" to something bigger than yourself by investing enthusiasm and passion to generate and grow this connection.

The more similar we are, the more likely we are to create a bond. This is good in that with stronger bonds we get more similarity of thought and collaboration. However, high degrees of similarity also can be a challenge, in that similar people are less likely to consider creative solutions outside of their current comfort levels.

The aim is to achieve the best of both worlds: To generate an environment where people engage in open ways to share knowledge and collaborate more effectively, but at the same time can open divergent approaches to thinking to derive innovation. There must be sufficient trust to have a sense of identity within the community, while people can also constructively challenge each other.

Creating a Safe-Fail Environment to Build Trust

The more you trust someone the more you will share with them. The more you share knowledge, the more collaborative co-creation of new knowledge happens, which is the fuel for innovation and performance. So there is a direct and tangible incentive to foster a safe environment that is conducive to building trust. I discussed a safe-fail environment earlier in this book. The concept was created by David Snowden, as a deliberate reversal of the traditional fail-safe mindset. Fail-safe is a risk-averse mentality that strives to remove all risk before actions are taken. It is appropriate to some high-risk, high-consequence industries such as space travel. However, this mindset is very stifling to innovation and slows down achievement. Safe-fail in contrast is the mindset in which people are encouraged to take risks and make small failures before they become larger errors. Leadership that enables safe-fail has a growth mindset[4] and operates more like Agile[5] approaches. The philosophy is that people and teams who quickly find the failure points can evolve the products, projects, and services more quickly to enhance them within shorter cycles and accelerate performance. Customer feedback can be more easily incorporated into continuous improvement as the development cycles are shorter and more flexible.

The challenge is that genuine trust takes time to build and mature but only moments to destroy. Once trust has been broken, it is very hard to rebuild and rarely returns to previous levels. People are social beings whose relationships at all levels and of all types are based on trust. A lack of trust will cause a poor culture that reduces performance. To be a KNOWledge SUCCESSion leader you need to proactively create a behavioral environment in which people feel safe to share and safe to fail. This means providing a high degree of freedom and fostering a no-blame culture. Leaders benefit by being a role model, sharing their own mistakes and highlighting what they learn from good and bad experiences.

In this book, I have tried to explain that being aware of what KNOWledge SUCCESSion is and why it is important to sustained success will assist you and those around you to be more effective and efficient. Acting on the interdependencies between the many aspects of leading others discussed in these chapters will make you a role model. These principles apply to everything in your professional and personal life. I have continued to use these principles in my own life and have benefited in many ways. The most important principle is being comfortable with who I am and why I do what I do and with whom I choose to collaborate to co-create new knowledge and generate value.

Contributor Case Study

Brigitte Carbonneau, Business Strategy Director, Cirque du Soleil, Canada

Cirque du Soleil's Approach to Talent Retention Challenges

Touring as performing artists at the highest level is a very demanding business. While "running away with the circus" may sound romantic, it is actually very tough work, physically and mentally, and requires the very best of talent, dedication, and passion. This is especially the case at Cirque du Soleil, where absolute amazing performance is expected every day by the most discerning of clients.

It takes a special kind of person to thrive under this constant pressure to perform. They need to be highly talented and be able to engage with a whole team of other highly talented artists and support staff. Yet, despite these challenges, Cirque du Soleil has to find creative ways to maintain his turnover as low as possible. I believe there are many interdependent reasons that explain our turnover rate. In addition to a highly sought after brand, we proactively build a participative culture and engage our people (on stage and off) to be their best. There are specific actions that we put in place at a certain moment of our history with the real intention of diminishing the turnover between employees and artists.

As an example, there were unexpected challenges we experienced when we first toured Europe in 1995. We underestimated the preparation to deal with cultural shock, language issues, local labor laws, and mentality and staff members were actively leaving. Reflecting on these helped us to prepare for subsequent visits and also for our first venture into Asia-Pacific in 1999.

For Asia-Pacific Tour (APT) once the staff and artists were hired, we prepared a "tour camp," to increase their adaptability in this territory and build relationships. We increased their awareness about the culture, organized cultural awareness and languages courses (basic Japanese and Chinese), offered sushi class, and hosted an expert in cultural differences informing us about the Asian cultures in a special presentation. Together, we enjoyed a film from the late Steve Irwin about dangerous animals in Australia. We transformed their fears into curiosity. We made everything possible, within our budget, to stimulate interest about the culture we were going to be living in. The objective was to make sure the employees and artists were focusing on their jobs, on making sure that the show will go on, while mitigating stresses and reducing irritating factors. The staff was composed of Asian, Australian, and Canadian and the chemistry these activities developed between the team was evident, making the investment highly productive and the culture participative and inclusive, even though our backgrounds, ethics, and values were different. There was a better understanding of each other and the integration went smoothly.

The success of this amazed us, on stage and off! After a full year of touring in Asia-Pacific delivering demanding but exciting shows, we did not have a single resignation among staff or artists. Even after two years, the turnover rate in this team was the lowest we experienced at that time for touring environment. The money we invested in our tour camp was the best investment we could have made. This engagement approach builds teams that appreciate their differences to enhance relationships, builds collective passion and mutual trust, stimulates pride in our product, and improves overall performance for everyone involved, audiences included.

Reflective Activities and Additional Learning Resources for the Curious Executive and Student:

Applying this learning in practice.

1. Create a stakeholder list for a project or initiative you are doing or are considering implementing. This can be as simple as a spreadsheet or table (or even the output of a conversation recorded on a flip chart or the output from the stakeholder activity in Chapter 5). Discuss your impression of the stakeholders with others to share perspectives

on likely stakeholder impacts on the project. Review this list regularly throughout your initiative and consider which stakeholders are most influential at which stages.

2. Explore a range of communities and find one to examine (consider face to face and virtual social media options in areas of your current capabilities and interests for you and your development needs). Join one community you believe you can contribute value to and get value from. Assess over time the value you gain against the effort you invest. Consider both the intangible and tangible impacts of what you learned to yourself and the community. How were you influenced as a stakeholder of this group and how did you influence stakeholders, within and beyond community, as a result of your participation? If one community is not generating mutual value after some time, explore another.

3. Write a pitch for your initiative and present it in less than three minutes to a target audience (or practice this in a role play to refine before doing it with the real stakeholder). There are many useful instruction videos on how to develop and deliver a pitch available. Figure 12.2 will be helpful in thinking about the approach. The approach I encourage my postgraduate students to follow is to focus on these key aspects in this order:

Opening impact: Is the opening statements compelling the target audience to listen?

Connectedness: Does the pitch flow in a logical manner, leading the audience through a plausible story?

Solution fit: Is the range of options appropriate for the situation and their context?

Presence: How are the presenters showing passion for their recommendations? Do they create credibility and confidence as well as demonstrate control?

Conclusion: Does the pitch finish with impact and the whole process flow to create a desire to engage?

Additional learning resources:

www.intelligentanswers.com.au/KnowledgeSuccession

Postscript

The Quest for Seasoned Knowledge-Informed Project Leaders

The ever-evolving field of Knowledge Management (KM) has been maturing for over 40 years. Many of us who were early thought leaders have been patiently awaiting a time when seasoned, credentialed project leads could handle the complex requirements of managing KM projects and initiatives. The quest for performance-related results, lessons learned, and knowledge nuggets has been a long or arduous search.

KNOWledge SUCCESSion offers many significant and critical insights into how knowledge-based projects can be more successful. Dr. Shelley is one of those mystical individuals who understand the alchemy underlying any KM initiative, where the executive sponsors and business champions wish to turn base metals into organizational gold. Arthur is not a dreamer; he is a scholarly practitioner whose pragmatic approach guides a team to success through a rigorous, disciplined, organized, and workable governance structure. As a practicing Rosicrucian, I am continually amazed at how the science, art, and craft of alchemy is materializing within our rarified knowledge-based enterprises. If ever there was a time when our enterprises required the use of a *"lapis philosophorum"* (Philosopher's Stone) that could transform the lead and mercury in our organizations into a golden state, it is now!

Private, public, and nonprofit organizations exhibit a paucity in leadership skills to "get things done." Too often, organizations are stressing politics over performance results and the world around us suffers immensely. *Magnum Opus* is a term within alchemy that describes the process of taking *prima materia* and transmuting it into the elusive *lapis philosophorum*. The transformational process is based upon individual transmutation, which eventually can accumulate into group, team, and organizational transmutation.

In *KNOWledge SUCCESSion*, we learn how organizational transformational can encompass the range of alchemical processes that are required to transmute the crude metal of our enterprises into increased shareholder value, improved performance management results, and the construction of competitive business value.

Dom Pernety's ***Dictionnaire mytho-hermétique*** (1744) provides us with a "cook book" for the 12 basic alchemical processes that comprise transmutation. We do not have the space in this postscript to connect each process to the work undertaken by Arthur to inform and credential his constituents. Nonetheless, my experiences in the areas of KM, gamification, and simulations highlight the value this can bring. I challenge readers to categorize the sections of Arthur's text in terms of these processes and send their list to me. Anyone who can get all twelve correct, I will send an award of more than insignificant value and announce the winners on my website.

Michael Sutton, PhD
Chief Gamification Officer and Chief Knowledge
Officer FUNIFICATION LLC

Notes

Chapter 1

1. Weick and Sutcliffe (2011).
2. Shelley (2009).
3. Petch (1998).
4. Hagel and Brown (2005).
5. Denning (2007).
6. Snowden and Boone (2007).
7. Covey and Merrill (2008).
8. Robinson (2011).
9. Shelley (2007).
10. Shelley (2011).
11. Morgan (2006).
12. Morris and Ma (2014).
13. Snowden and Boone (2007).
14. Klakegg et al. (2010).
15. Bennet et al. (2015).
16. Sage, Dainty, and Brookes (2014).
17. Amabile (1998).
18. Amabile and Kramer (2011).
19. See deeper discussion of outputs and outcomes in Chapter 7.
20. Checkland (1981).

Chapter 2

1. Godin (2012).
2. Pfeffer and Sutton (2000).
3. O'Reilly and Tushman (2002).
4. Adapted from Shelley (2009).
5. Morris (2011).
6. PMI (2013).
7. Müller and Turner (2010).
8. Hill (2013).
9. Brown (2014).
10. Kloppenborg and Laning (2012).
11. Vartanian and Mandel (2011).

12. Turner (2015).
13. Klien (2014).
14. Checkland (1981).
15. Winter and Szczepanek (2009).
16. Shelley (2009).
17. Kerzner (2014).
18. Leonard and Swap (2005).
19. Wiseman and Mckeown (2010).
20. Senge (2006).
21. Shelley (2009).
22. Brabham (2013).

Chapter 3

1. Pease (2008).
2. SAI Global (2015).
3. Innosight (2012).
4. Bertolini, Duncan, and Waldeck (2015).
5. Johnson (2011).
6. Knowles (1980).
7. Snowden and Boone (2007).
8. Liedtka, King, and Bennett (2013).
9. Radboud University Nijmegen (2014).
10. Ramachandran and Rogers-Ramachandran (2005).

Chapter 4

1. Sinek (2011).
2. Shelley (2010).
3. Senge (2006).
4. De Bono (1999).
5. Cooperrider, Whitney, and Stavros (2008).
6. Brown (2009).
7. Jung (2006).
8. Amabile and Kramer (2011).

Chapter 5

1. Baugh (2015).
2. Baugh (2015).

3. 70:20:10 forum (2016).
4. Knowles, Holton, and Swanson (2011).
5. McIntosh (2010).

Chapter 6

1. Shelley (2009).
2. Schön (1987).
3. McIntosh (2010).
4. Gibbs (1988).
5. Dewey (1933).
6. Hay (2007).
7. Norlander-Case, Reagan, and Case (1999).
8. Shelley (2012).
9. Argyris and Schön (1991).
10. Gladwell (2008).
11. Lesca and Lesca (2011).
12. Duhigg (2012).
13. Goleman (2013).
14. Gruenter and Whitaker (2015).

Chapter 7

1. Schmidt and Rosenberg (2014).
2. Leonard and Strauss (1997).
3. de Bono (1985).
4. Gurteen (2014).
5. Goffee and Jones (2015).
6. Collins (2001).
7. Greenleaf (2002).
8. Leonard and Swap (2005).
9. Thomas and Brown (2011).
10. Valkenburg and Dzubak (2012).
11. Bloom (1954).
12. Jung (1964).
13. Duhigg (2012).

Chapter 8

1. Krajewski (2014).
2. Gaughen (1998).

3. Collins (2004).
4. Christensen (2003).
5. Kim and Mauborgne (2005).
6. Lakoff and Johnson (1980).
7. Morgan (2006).
8. Shelley (2007).
9. Winter and Szczepanek (2009).
10. Sala (2003).
11. Checkland and Poulter (2006).
12. Sala (2003).

Chapter 9

1. Australian Research Council (2015).
2. Weiner (2016).
3. Stepper (2015).
4. Tufte (2001).
5. King (2015).
6. Rosling (2006).
7. McCandless (2010).
8. Simon (2014).
9. RSA (2016).
10. Agerbeck (2012).
11. Lankow, Ritchie, and Crooks (2012).

Chapter 10

1. Hofstede (2001).
2. Goleman (2011).
3. Shelley (2007).
4. Shelley (2011).

Chapter 11

1. Dweck (2012).
2. Medina (2014).
3. Doidge (2008).
4. Luo (2007).
5. Crisp (2015).

Chapter 12

1. Aristotle (350 BCE).
2. Shelley (2009).
3. Weiner (2016).
4. Dweck (2012).
5. Morris and Ma (2014).

References

70:20:10 Forum. 2016. Retrieved from www.702010forum.com

Agerbeck, B. 2012. *The Graphic Facilitator's Guide: How to Use Your Listening, Thinking and Drawing Skills to Make Meaning.* Chicago, IL. Loosetooth.com

Amabile, T.M. September–October 1998. *How to Kill Creativity*, 76–87. Boston, MA: Harvard Business School Publishing.

Amabile, T.M., and S.J. Kramer. 2011. *The Progress Principle: Using Small Wins to Ignite Joy, Engagement, and Creativity at Work.* Cambridge, MA: Harvard Business Press Books.

Argyris, C., and D. Schön. 1996. *Organizational Learning II: Theory, Method and Practice.* Reading, MA: Addison-Wesley.

Aristotle. 350 BCE. *Rhetoric.* Translated by W.R. Roberts 1924.

Australian Research Council. 2015. "Excellence in Research for Australia." Retrieved from www.arc.gov.au/era-2015

Baugh, A. 2015. *Stakeholder Engagement: The Game Changer for Program Management.* Boca Raton, FL: CRC Press.

Bennet, A., D. Bennet, and R. Turner. 2015. *Expanding the Self: The Intelligent Complex Adaptive Learning System.* Frost, WV: MQI Press.

Bertolini, M., D. Duncan, and A. Waldeck. December 2015. "Knowing When to Reinvent: Detecting Marketplace "Fault Lines" is the Key to Building the Case for Preemptive Change." *Harvard Business Review*, 91, no. 12, pp. 90–101.

Bloom, B.S. 1956–1964. *Taxonomy of Educational Objectives.* New York: David McKay Company Inc.

Brabham, D. 2013. *Crowdsourcing.* Cambridge, MA: MIT Press.

Brown, J. 2014. *The Handbook of Program Management: How to Facilitate Project Success with Optimal Program Management.* New York: McGraw-Hill Education.

Brown, T. 2009. *Change by Design: How Design Thinking Transforms Organizations and Inspires Innovation.* New York: HarperBusiness.

Checkland, P. 1981. *Systems Thinking, Systems Practice.* New York: John Wiley and Sons Inc.

Checkland, P., and J. Poulter. 2006. *Learning for Action. A Short Definitive Account of Soft Systems Methodology for Practitioners, Teachers and Students.* New York: John Wiley and Sons Inc.

Christensen, C.M. 2003. *The Innovator's Solution: Creating and Sustaining Successful Growth.* Cambridge, MA: Harvard Business Press.

Collins, J.C. 2001. *Good to Great: Why Some Companies make the Leap ... and Others Don't*. New York: HarperBusiness.

Cooperrider, D.L., D. Whitney, and J.M. Stavros. 2008. *The Appreciative Inquiry Handbook: For Leaders of Change*. San Francisco, CA: Berrett-Koehler Publishers.

Covey, S.M., and R.R. Merrill. 2008. *The SPEED of Trust: The One Thing That Changes Everything*. New York: Free Press.

Crisp, R. 2015. *The Social Brain, How Diversity Made the Modern Mind*. London: Robinson.

de Bono, E. 1999. *Six Thinking Hats*. Boston, MA: Back Bay Books.

Denning, S. 2007. *The Secret Language of Leadership: How Leaders Inspire Action Through Narrative*. San Francisco, CA: Jossey-Bass.

Dewey, J. 1933. *How We Think: A Restatement of the Relation of Reflective Thinking to the Educative Process*. Boston: Houghton Mifflin.

Doidge, N. 2008. *The Brain That Changes Itself: Stories of Personal Triumph from the Frontiers of Brain Science*. London: Penguin Books.

Duhigg, C. 2012. *The Power of Habit: Why We Do What We Do in Life and Business*. New York: Random House.

Dweck, C. 2012. *Mindset. How You Can Fulfill Your Potential*. London: Robinson.

Gaughen, P. December 1998. "Structural Inefficiency in the Early Twentieth Century: Studies in the Aluminum and Incadescent Lamp Markets." *Social Science* 610.

Gibbs, G. 1988. *Learning by Doing: A Guide to Teaching and Learning Methods*. Oxford, UK: Further Education Unit, Oxford Polytechnic.

Gladwell, M. 2008. *Outliers: The Story of Success*. New York, NY: Little, Brown and Company.

Godin, S. 2012. *Whatcha Gonna do with That Duck?* London: Portfolio/Penguin.

Goffee, R., and G. Jones. 2015. *Why Should Anyone Be Led by You? What It Takes to Be an Authentic*. Boston, MA: Harvard Business School Press.

Goleman, D. 2011. *Social Intelligence: The New Science of Human Relationships*. London: Hutchinson.

Goleman, D. 2013. *What Makes a Leader: Why Emotional Intelligence Matters*. Florence, MA: More Than Sound.

Greenleaf, R. 2002. *Servant Leadership: A Journey into the Nature of Legitimate Power and Greatness*. Mahwah, NJ: Paulist Press.

Gruenert, S., and T. Whitaker. 2015. *School Culture Rewired: How to Define, Assess, and Transform it*. Alexandria, VA: Association for Supervision and Curriculum Development.

Gurteen, D. 2014. "Organizational Conversation." *iKNOW Magazine*, 4, no. 1, Special Edition.

Hagel, J., and J. Brown. 2005. *The Only Sustainable Edge. Why Business Strategy Depends on Productive Friction and Dynamic Specialization*. Cambridge, MA: Harvard Business Review Press.

Hay, J. 2007. *Reflective Practice and Supervision for Coaches*. New York: McGraw Hill.

Hill, G. 2013. *The Complete Project Management Office Handbook*. 3rd ed. Boca Raton, FL: Auerbach Publications.

Hofstede, G. 2001. *Culture's Consequences. Comparing Values, Behaviors, Institutions, and Organizations Across Nations*. 2nd ed. London: Sage.

Innosight. 2012. "Creative Destruction Whips through Corporate America." Retrieved from www.innosight.com/innovation-resources/strategy-innovation/creative-destruction-whips-through-corporate-america.cfm

Johnson, S. 2011. *Where Good Ideas Come From. The Natural History of Innovation*. London: Riverhead Books.

Jung, C. 1964. *Man and His Symbols*. New York: Doubleday Hardcover.

Jung, C.G. 2006 (reissued). *The Undiscovered Self*. New York: Signet.

Kerzner, H. 2014. *Project Recovery: Case Studies and Techniques for Overcoming Project Failure*. Hoboken, NY: John Wiley and Sons.

Kim, W., and R. Mauborgne. 2005. *Blue Ocean Strategy. How to Create Uncontested Market Space and Make the Competition Irrelevant*. Boston, MA: Harvard Business School Press.

King, R. 2015. *Visual Storytelling with D3: An introduction to Data Visualization in Javascript*. Upper Saddle River, NJ: Addison-Wesley.

Klakegg, O.J., T. Williams, D.H.T. Walker, B. Andersen, and M.O. Morten. 2010. *Early Warning Signs in Complex Projects*. Newton Square, PA: Project Management Institute.

Klein, G. 2014. *Seeing What Others Don't. The Remarkable Ways We Gain Insights*. London: Nicholas Brealey Publishing.

Kloppenborg, T., and L. Laning. 2012. *Strategic Leadership of Portfolio and Project Management*. New York: Business Expert Press.

Knowles, M.S. 1980. *The Modern Practice of Adult Education. Andragogy Versus Pedagogy*. Cambridge: Englewood Cliffs Prentice Hall.

Knowles, M.S., E.F. Holton, and R.A. Swanson. 2011. *The Adult Learner. The Definitive Classic in Adult Education and Human Resource Development*. Oxford, UK: Butterworth-Heinemann.

Krajewski, M. 2014. "The Great Lightbulb Conspiracy. The Phoebus Cartel Engineered a Shorter-Lived Lightbulb and Gave Birth to Planned Obsolescence." Retrieved from http://spectrum.ieee.org/geek-life/history/the-great-lightbulb-conspiracy/

Lakoff, G., and M. Johnson. 1980. *Metaphors We Live By*. Chicago: University of Chicago Press.

Lankow, J., J. Ritchie, and R. Crooks. 2012. *Infographics: The Power of Visual Storytelling.* Hoboken, NJ: John Wiley and Sons.

Leonard, D., and S. Straus. 1997. "Putting Your Company's Whole Brain to Work." *Harvard Business Review* 75, no. 4, pp. 110–21.

Leonard, D., and W. Swap. 2005. *Deep Smarts: How to Cultivate and Transfer Enduring Business.* Boston, MA: Harvard Business School Press.

Lesca, H., and N. Lesca. 2011. *Weak Signals for Strategic Intelligence: Anticipation Tool for Managers.* Hoboken, NJ: Wiley & Sons.

Liedtka, J., A. King, and K. Bennett. 2013. *Solving Problems with Design Thinking. Ten Stories of What Works.* New York: Columbia University Press.

Luo, Y. 2007. *Guanxi and Business.* Singapore: World Scientific Publishing.

McCandless, D. 2010. "The Beauty of Data Visualization." Retrieved from www.ted.com/talks/lang/en/david_mccandless_the_beauty_of_data_visualization.html

McIntosh, P. 2010. *Action Research and Reflective Practice. Creative and Visual Methods to Facilitate Reflection and Learning.* London, NY: Routledge.

Medina, J. 2014. *Brain Rules. 12 Principles for Surviving and Thriving at Work, Home and School.* London: Scribe.

Morgan, G. 2006. *Images of Organization.* London: Sage Publications.

Morris, L., and M. Ma. 2014. *Agile Innovation: The Revolutionary Approach to Accelerate Success, Inspire Engagement, and Ignite Creativity.* Hoboken, NJ: John Wiley and Sons.

Morris, P.W., ed. 2011. "A Brief History of Project Management." In *The Oxford Handbook on Project Management,* 15–36. Oxford: Oxford University Press.

Müller, R., and J.R. Turner. 2010. *Project-Oriented Leadership.* Surrey: Gower Publishing Limited

Norlander-Case, K., T. Reagan, and C. Case. 1999. *The Professional Teacher.* San Francisco, CA: Jossey-Bass.

O'Reilly, C., and M. Tushman. 2002. *Winning Through Innovation: A Practical Guide to Leading Organizational Change and Renewal.* Boston, MA: Harvard Business School Publishing.

Pease, A. 2008. *Questions are the Answers.* Bhopal: Manjul Publishing House.

Petch, G. October 1998. "The Cost of Lost Knowledge." *Knowledge Management,* pp. 45–48.

Pfeffer, J., and R.I. Sutton. 2000. *The Knowing-Doing Gap: How Smart Companies Turn Knowledge Into Action.* Boston, MA: Harvard Business School Publishing.

PMI (Project Management Institute). 2013. *A Guide to the Project Management Body of Knowledge: PMBOK Guide.* 5th ed. Newtown Square: Project Management Institute.

Radboud University Nijmegen. 2014. "Brain Fills Gaps to Produce a Likely Picture." Retrieved from www.sciencedaily.com/releases/2014/06/140627094551.htm

Ramachandran, V., and D. Rogers-Ramachandran. 2005. "Mind the Gap The Brain, Like Nature, Abhors a Vacuum." Retrieved from www.scientificamerican.com/article/mind-the-gap/

Robinson, K. 2011. *Out of Our Minds. Learning To Be Creative.* 2nd ed. Chichester, UK: Capstone Publishing Ltd.

Rosling, H. 2006. "The Best Stats You Have Ever Seen." Retrieved from www.ted.com/talks/hans_rosling_shows_the_best_stats_you_ve_ever_seen

RSA (Royal Society of Arts). 2016. "RSA Animate." Retrieved from www.thersa.org/discover/videos/rsa-animate/

Sage, D., A. Dainty, and N. Brookes. 2014. "A Critical Argument in Favor of Theoretical Pluralism: Project Failure and The Many and Varied Limitations of Project Management." *International Journal of Project Management* 32, no. 3, pp. 544–55.

SAI Global, 2015. "Business Excellence Awards." Retrieved from www.saiglobal.com/improve/excellencemodels/businessexcellenceframework/

Sala, F. September 2003. "Laughing All the Way To The Bank." *Harvard Business Review* 81, no. 9, pp. 16–17.

Schmidt, E., and J. Rosenberg. 2014. *How Google Works.* Paris: Hachette.

Schön, D.A. 1987. *Educating the Reflective Practitioner.* San Francisco, CA: Jossey-Bass.

Senge, P. 2006. *The Fifth Discipline: The Art & Practice of The Learning Organization.* New York: Random House Ltd.

Shelley, A.W. 2007. *The Organizational Zoo A Survival Guide to Workplace Behavior.* Fairfield, CT: Aslan Publishing.

Shelley, A.W. 2009. *Being a Successful Knowledge Leader.* North Sydney: Ark Group.

Shelley, A.W. 2010. "Conversations That Matter." Retrieved from www.organizationalzoo.com/blog/2010/01/conversations-that-matter/

Shelley, A.W. 2011. "Creative Metaphor as a Tool for Stakeholder Influence." In *Advising Upwards: A Framework for Understanding and Engaging Senior Management Stakeholders,* ed. L. Bourne. Aldershot, UK: Gower Publishing Ltd.

Shelley, A.W. 2012. *Metaphor as a Means to Constructively Influence Behavioural Interactions in Project Teams.* (PhD thesis). Melbourne, Australia: RMIT University.

Simon, P. 2014. *The Visual Organization: Data Visualization, Big Data, and the Quest for Better Decisions.* Hoboken, NJ: John Wiley and Sons.

Sinek, S. 2011. *Start with Why: How Great Leaders Inspire Everyone to Take Action.* New York: Portfolio/Penguin.

Snowden, D., and M. Boone. 2007. "A Leaders Framework for Decision Making." *Harvard Business Review* 85, no. 11, pp. 68–76.

Stepper, J. 2015. *Working Out Loud. For a Better Career and Life.* New York: Ikigai Press.

Thomas, D., and J.S. Brown. 2011. *A New Culture of Learning: Cultivating the Imagination for a World of Constant Change.* Seattle, WA: CreateSpace.

Tufte, E.R. 2001. *The Visual Display of Quantitative Information.* 2nd ed. Cheshire, CN: Graphics Press.

Turner, C. 2015. "Government in £9 Million Payout After Single Letter Blunder Causes Business to Collapse." *London Telegraph.* Retrieved from www.telegraph.co.uk/news/uknews/law-and-order/11372343/Government-in-9-million-payout-after-single-letter-blunder-causes-business-to-collapse.html

Valkenburg, J., and C. Dzubak. 2012. *The Engaged Mind: Cognitive Skills and Learning.* Seattle, WA: CreateSpace.

Vartanian, O., and D. Mandel. eds. 2011. *Neuroscience of Decision Making. Contemporary Topics in Cognitive Neuroscience.* New York: Psychology Press.

Weick, K.E., and K.M. Sutcliffe. 2011. *Managing the Unexpected. Resilient Performance in an Age of Uncertainty.* Hoboken, NJ: John Wiley and Sons Inc.

Weiner, E. 2016. *The Geography of Genius. A Search for the World's Most Creative Places from Ancient Athens to Silicon Valley.* New York: Simon and Shuster.

Winter, M., and T. Szczepanek. 2009. *Images of Projects.* Farnham, UK: Gower.

Wiseman, L., and G. Mckeown. 2010. *Multipliers: How the Best Leaders Make Everyone Smarter.* New York: HarperCollins Publishers.

Index

OTHER TITLES IN OUR PORTFOLIO AND PROJECT MANAGEMENT COLLECTION

Timothy J. Kloppenborg, Editor

- *Making Projects Sing: A Musical Perspective of Project Management* by Raji Sivaraman and Chris Wilson
- *Agile Project Management for Business Transformation Success* by Milan Frankl and Paul Paquette
- *Leveraging Business Analysis for Project Success* by Vicki James
- *Project Portfolio Management: A Model for Improved Decision Making* by Clive N. Enoch
- *Project Management Essentials* by Kathryn Wells and Timothy J. Kloppenborg
- *The Agile Edge: Managing Projects Effectively Using Agile Scrum* by Brian Vanderjack
- *Project Teams: A Structured Development Approach* by Vittal S. Anantatmula
- *Attributes of Project-Friendly Enterprises* by Vittal S. Anantatmula and Parviz F. Rad
- *Stakeholder-led Project Management: Changing the Way We Manage Projects* by Louise Worsley

Announcing the Business Expert Press Digital Library

Concise e-books business students need for classroom and research

This book can also be purchased in an e-book collection by your library as

- a one-time purchase,
- that is owned forever,
- allows for simultaneous readers,
- has no restrictions on printing, and
- can be downloaded as PDFs from within the library community.

Our digital library collections are a great solution to beat the rising cost of textbooks. E-books can be loaded into their course management systems or onto students' e-book readers.
The **Business Expert Press** digital libraries are very affordable, with no obligation to buy in future years. For more information, please visit **www.businessexpertpress.com/librarians**. To set up a trial in the United States, please email **sales@businessexpertpress.com**.

CPSIA information can be obtained
at www.ICGtesting.com
Printed in the USA
FFOW03n2231191216
30401FF

9 781631 571589